Crystal Lake
a three picnic day

Roy Marshall with Janielle Kenworthy

Aventine Press

Copyright © 2012, Roy Marshall
First Edition

Without limiting the rights under copyright reserved above, no part of this publication may be reproduced, stored in or introduced into a retrieval system, or transmitted, in any form or by any means (electronic, mechanical, photocopying, recording, or otherwise), without the prior written permission of the copyright owner of this book.

Published by Aventine Press
55 East Emerson St.
Chula Vista CA, 91911
www.aventinepress.com

ISBN: 1-59330-774-8
ALL RIGHTS RESERVED

CONTENTS

Chapter 1	A generous amount of his final twenty or thirty years was spent in conversation	Page 3
Chapter 2	Cass County, it seemed, had everything but a lake	Page 9
Chapter 3	Captain Huffy's heroism was for naught, and the Mary Ann sank	Page 13
Chapter 4	Constable Bates weight his options, then bade the lady a good evening	Page 17
Chapter 5	The law was clear as spring water—baseball could not be played in Lewis on Sunday	Page 29
Chapter 6	Black walnut timber is sure to be of great value in the construction of aeroplanes	Page 37
Chapter 7	He was sick and he was going blind	Page 43
Chapter 8	Whatever happens we will still have Crystal Lake. It cannot be taken from us	Page 51
Chapter 9	The town marshal, a dog in hot pursuit, took refuge on John Jayberg's front porch	Page 63
Chapter 10	They would, however, designate it as a state if the land was donated	Page 67
Chapter 11	The Lewis semi-pro maidens thumped Marne, 21-7	Page 75
Chapter 12	Rowdiness would not be tolerated any time of the day or night	Page 79

Chapter 13	Upson died, milk bucket at his side, at the age of 62	Page 85
Chapter 14	King was outraged when he realized the wrong tooth had been extracted	Page 95
Chapter 15	The state man left in a huff	Page 109
Chapter 16	After two years of Riley P. Clark the state was moved to action	Page 117
Chapter 17	For all things, Young concluded, there is a season	Page 123
Chapter 18	. . . desires to be free and clear of maintenance of certain lands in Cass County	Page 129
Epilogue		Page 135
Dedication		Page 137
Credits		Page 139

Forward

The walk wasn't a long one, a couple of hundred yards, but much of it difficult because what once had been a distinct and well-worn path through a grove of oak and hickory was now eroded, clogged with undergrowth, branches, fallen trees. On my left was the base of a steep, in places sheer, sandstone bluff. On the right was the lakeshore. The murky water, that day in mid- March, seemed cold and foreboding.

I climbed over the trunk of a soft maple, sank ankle deep in mud, slogged through what was now just a reminder of an object I'd seen only in photographs—the steel pipe driven over a century ago into the bluff, a pipe from which constantly flowing spring water, said by Lewis doctors to be a healthful tonic, attracted people from far away.

Skirting a rotting picnic table that had probably been pushed over the precipice by vandals, stepping over beer cans pale with age, broken bottles, plastic milk jugs crumbling like eggshells, I encountered two lengths of twisted metal pipe; pipe that had once carried water from the spring box Chet Woodward built to hydrants above. Nearby, although I could not pinpoint the location, had been a stairway extending from lakeside to campgrounds until being demolished sixty-odd years ago.

One hundred and two steps. Fifty steps, I'd been told, to the landing then fifty-two more to the top. Children counted them, often aloud, running all the way. As they grew older and went slower they continued counting. Fifty steps and stop at the landing, rest a bit, then fifty-two more.

I was not looking for anything in particular, although finding the spring box allowed for a more precise estimation of the location of the original lake, the pavilion, the bandstand, other long ago attractions on land that is now under water.

Initials were there, carved in stone near where the stairway landing had been, just as Deb Herbert remembered. Most were no longer legible, faded and weathered and covered with a fine film of the same stubborn moss and lichen that grows on the north side of marble tombstones. Failing to decipher one set of initials I tried others; some with success, some not. I'd been told the building of the new lake had resulted in the obliteration of these initials, but this is not entirely the case. Many remain, some probably dating to when this place became a well-known stop-over for white travelers in the mid 1800s.

I was about to leave when I saw, high on the bluff perhaps seventy-five feet west of the spring box, letters that appeared sharp, although too distant to read.

Even in my youth the climb would have been a challenge. Halfway up, clinging to a sturdy vine, boots unable to gain traction, I realized a wiser option would be to quit and return with binoculars. But I was halfway, and above me a scrub tree reached out from where it had taken root in a crevice, and up I went. The letters, perhaps because they were high enough for the sun to find them, were worn but distinct, not shrouded in moss. Taking pen and paper, not trusting memory, I wondered how difficult the carving had been from this lofty and precarious position. Had he or she been lowered by rope from above? Perhaps stood on the shoulders of a friend who was on the shoulders of another, and another? Simply brought a ladder? I wondered about the event, the camaraderie, the weather the day someone had inscribed: 'TLG 09'

Although I came not sure of what I was looking for, I'd found it. Just over a century ago TLG had been where I was. At that time the focal point of an amusement park teeming with people was here, at the base of this bluff, a few feet from the waterslide, the pavilion vendors, the stairway from which visitors could turn and see it all. Then the Iowa Conservation Commission, encouraged by local conservationists and preservationists and sportsmen, made changes that resulted in this place becoming an all but inaccessible bog, a target for revelers on the high ground throwing trash.

The Crystal Lake "TLG" experienced in 1909 bore little resemblance to Cold Springs Park of today.

Chapter One

*A generous amount of his final twenty or thirty years
was devoted to conversation*

When Maxine Bode Dolch was eleven years old she and her sisters, Arlene Bode Jahnke and Betty Bode Thompson, had an amusement park in their back yard. Crystal Lake. Now ninety-one years old, Maxine speaks of the place with a smile and a tear. There was nothing else quite like it. The Bode girls remember warm summer days, a sparkling little lake with a bench in the center where bathers could sit in the sun, soaking their grey rented uniforms but rarely their hair, watching the bustle at the pavilion, children shrieking as they cannon-balled down the water-slide; swings, picnickers, skating rink and baseball games and music. Bands—some good and some less so—the calliope in the roller rink, glee clubs, tap dancers, accordion players. And of course there was the menagerie called 'Quinn's Zoo.'

The Bode family lived, for a time in the 1920s and early 30s, on the old Woodward place, the house Jehu and Jane Woodward built, that Chet and Belle were living in when Crystal Lake as the Bode girls knew it was created.

When Maxine Bode celebrated her eleventh birthday Belle Myers Woodward had been dead for fifteen years. Belle's eleventh birthday had been observed in 1863, probably without a celebration. That year the battle of Gettysburg was waged, part of it, on the Myers family farm. 50,000 men were shot, bayoneted or bludgeoned within a mile or two of her home. Before the carnage soldiers from both the north and south pillaged the Myers farm. Lean, hard-faced men in blue were there, then moved on. Soldiers in grey came, departed, each army groping for advantage, maneuvering for position. They slaughtered livestock, ripped out fences and tore down buildings for campfires, trampled crops and uprooted gardens. The soldiers called it foraging.

If Belle left an account of her memories of the war we find no record. In public she tended, like women of her day, to let her husband do the talking.

Her husband was glad to oblige. Daniel Winchester Woodward, who celebrated his eleventh birthday in a partially-completed cabin south of Lewis during the winter of 1856-57, thoroughly enjoyed talking. He lived ninety-six years, including well over two decades after he rented out the farm and moved to Lewis. A generous amount of his final twenty or thirty years was devoted to conversation.

Chet Woodward was an outgoing fellow who made, during his retirement years, the two-block walk to Lewis' business district every day the weather permitted. With Belle gone he took a meal or two at one of the town's restaurants. His favorite was a hamburger shop operated by a close friend, Karl McDonald. He had sons who were main street merchants. Chet dropped into the hardware store to chat, the feed store, spent a little time at the railroad depot. He liked sitting on a bench outside either of the town's groceries, strolling to the office of The Lewis Standard to visit with the editor, Charley Willey. Chet most enjoyed recalling times gone by. He did not have a wartime experience like Belle to relive. What he had was the lake and amusement park he and his family built.

Willey, as years passed, recounted in his newspaper some of his conversations with Chet Woodward. Most had to do with coming to Iowa as a ten-year-old boy, and always Crystal Lake.

Jehu and Jane Marshall Woodward and children arrived in Cass County in 1856. Traveling from their former home in Warren, Ohio, they took a route more pleasant, and expensive, than that taken by overland travelers. Loading their belongings, including a team of mules, onto a steamboat they enjoyed a leisurely cruise down the scenic Ohio River to the Mississippi, then to the junction with the Missouri and from there upstream to Kanesville (Council Bluffs).

Lafe Young (1848-1926) published the *Atlantic Telegraph*, later the *Des Moines Capital*, became state legislator, war correspondent, a friend of Teddy Roosevelt. He also wrote the 1877 History of Cass County. In this book he makes reference to Charles E. Woodward, who is apparently the first of that name to arrive in the county. As justice of the peace, Charles Woodward heard, in 1852, the county's first court case—a lawsuit involving a couple of peddlers. If and how Charles and Jehu were related we do not know, but it would not be surprising if Jehu, while living in Ohio, learned of the opportunity for cheap land in southwest Iowa from someone already here. Jehu was eligible to purchase, under the federal pre-emption act, up to 300 acres. This he did, acquiring the land in parcels over a period of years.

Jehu and Jane became owners of an interesting bit of real estate. The East Nishnabotna River, before being straightened, made a loop that cut a wide and leisurely swath through the southwest corner of their farm. The bluffs and springs were a hundred yards or so east of the easternmost point of this bend of the river.

Originating in the hills to the east, passing near the bluff and flowing into the Nishnabotna, was Deep Creek. Deep Creek was not often deep. But it drained several hundred acres of farmland and, following a heavy rain, was prone to leave its banks. The flooding potential of Deep Creek, and of the Nishnabota with its wide twists and turns that slowed the passage of water, increased as prairie grass was plowed under, removing expanses of sod and roots and tall foliage that held rainwater in check.

A quarter mile northeast of the bluff was a knobby hillside that, concealed by a thin layer of soil, contained a quantity of sandstone. Jehu Woodward did not "discover" the stone, although he's sometimes credited with doing so. A man named Jesters, identified in documents as "Squire" Jesters, quarried there before Woodward's arrival and, in fact, county records indicate the road from Lewis south was built to accommodate traffic to and from the quarry.

The Jehu Woodward farm had good points and bad. Having land on the other side of the river rendered that parcel of limited use. While the springs provided a year-round watering place for livestock, they also created a boggy marsh that could mire down a horse or cow. The bluff and surrounding area had ample timber for firewood, fence rails and buildings, and the flatland to the north and east of the river was rich soil, black and deep, capable of raising a fine crop. While a portion of the land was, when Deep Creek overflowed and the river backed up, susceptible to flooding, and thirty or forty acres around the springs too wooly for crops, Jehu Woodward had more than enough choice land to keep him busy.

The Woodwards appear to have done well. In addition to farming he took work as a carpenter. Jehu's income was further supplemented by the demand for sandstone. A good many foundations, along with several entire buildings, were erected of stone from his quarry. The most noted of these is the one west of the Nishnabotna built by the abolitionist, Reverend George Hitchcock. Sandstone from the Woodward farm, quarried and cut more than a century and a half ago, endures in the now restored structure that once was a key stop-over on the Underground Railroad.

One of the carpentry jobs Jehu undertook was re-roofing a hotel in Lewis. Henry Myers, deeply discouraged by the devastation his farm and family had endured during the Gettysburg battle, sold out and moved to Iowa . He arrived in 1867, acquired some farmland and the hotel, which later became a stage stop and inn, and was re-named "Pennsylvania House" for his home state. Jehu Woodward, accompanied by one of his sons, Chet, was working on the roof at the Pennsylvania House when they met Belle. Chet was then about twenty-two; Belle sixteen.

Jehu was 44 years old when he relocated to Iowa. Of his and Jane's children (seven were raised to adulthood; several others died young) only Chet became a farmer   Other sons went into business—merchants in Lewis, one a banker and another a druggist in Griswold—while the Woodward daughters married and followed their husbands.

In 1871 Daniel Winchester Woodward married Belle Jeannette Myers. They rented land a few miles south of the home place. The railroad that connected Atlantic with Red Oak created the town of Griswold in 1879. Chet was there, later recalled taking work as a foreman with a crew that built the first road from Griswold west to the Nishnabotna river. This was low-lying land, some of it marsh, and Chet learned to deal with the difficulties of grading and scraping in that terrain. The lesson would serve him well when he and his wife set out to build a lake.

Chet and Belle would buy the farm south of Lewis when his parents retired, and there they raised their family.

Chapter Two

Cass County, it seemed, had everything but a lake

By the summer of 1895 Cass County was a far different place than when Jane and Jehu arrived. The Atlantic Canning Company, claiming to be largest corn canning plant in the world, able to put up 80,000 cans of vegetables a day, was running at capacity. Atlantic also had a large starch plant, foundry, machine shops and jewelry stores. The Palace Livery at 504 South Walnut boasted the finest horses and rigs "to be had anywhere." The Mutual Benefit Building and Loan Company, located at the corner of 6th and Chestnut, did business all over the state. The Model Steam Laundry had locations in ten area towns. C.W. Harris ran a bakery at 307 Chestnut, a bakery with an oven capable of turning out 400 loaves of bread at a time. Mr. Harris also sold ice cream, oysters in season, and carried a good selection of cigars—some of them locally made. Levi Downs took a job as a clerk at the age of 16, learned the trade, and by 1896 his general mercantile store in Atlantic was the largest between Council Bluffs and Des Moines. Mrs. M.E. Howard, after twenty-five years in the millinery business in Des Moines, relocated to Atlantic. Her display of current styles offered the fair sex, according to an ad, "a scene approaching paradise." W.D. Blackwood, general proprietor of the Park Barber Shop and Bath Rooms at 518 Chestnut, advertised that he was both a practical and skilled tonsorial expert and employed only gentlemen of comparable abilities. James Jones was a dealer in farm machinery, buggies, stock feed, and manufactured the 'Jones five-horse plow and binder evener,' said by the Atlantic newspaper to be "a very handy and useful article." The C.E. Dackens Cigar Factory at 403½ Chestnut made the "La Flor de Clove," as fine a cigar as a man could get for a nickel. For those who could afford the best the "La Flor de Spain" sold for a dime.

In Lewis was the DeLean Cheese Plant, Allen's broom factory, a brick foundry, hotel, three doctors and two lawyers. The Citizen's State Bank had a competitor. Okell & Weaver had a general store offering the latest in fine undergarments—including the heralded "hipless corset." J.H. Baker sold ice, groceries, and sausage of his own making. When the fire department bought a new length of hose Baker was accused, probably unjustly, of using the old hose to stuff bologna.

Molly Mills was proprietor of a millinery emporium that carried a line of flowered, feathered hats guaranteed to turn heads. Lewis had both electricity and telephones, with lines strung on poles that were, in places, too close together. When a high voltage line brushed against a telephone wire, which happened from time to time, every phone down the line jangled, causing operators at central to yank plugs and fume and deal with dozens of people wanting to know who'd tried to call them up. These events were called "a hello of a time."

Lewis had two liveries—one would become a garage and automobile dealer—feed stores and the Joyce Lumber Company, which offered free delivery. Similar businesses and professional services were found in towns and at crossroads throughout the area.

And, when not at work, there was plenty for people to do in their leisure. Every town had a park, some had several—most with bandstands, shade trees, picnic area and playgrounds—places intended for family reunions, patriotic celebrations, revival meetings, gatherings of business and fraternal organizations. Opera houses featured performances ranging from educational lectures to evangelists to coarse, cross-dressing parodies and black-face comedy. An opera house might even, on rare occasions, have an opera. The county fairgrounds stayed busy all summer.

If we were to take a balloon ride over Cass County during the 1890s we'd see hundreds of farmsteads that are now corn fields, and we'd see more horse racing tracks than high school football fields. Southwest Iowa, in the 1890s, was the home of Alix, a smallish mare who was then the fastest trotter in the world. Had she been foaled and stabled in New

York or Chicago or anywhere in Kentucky she'd also have been the most celebrated. Even so, at a time when harness racing was the king of sports, her fans came from far away to see her, to touch her velvet nose. Carl Sandberg wrote and published a verse about his memories of Alix.

Cass County, it seemed, had everything but a lake.

Belle Myers Woodward was in her 44th year, a farmer's wife, the mother of 11 children—the youngest just two years old—when the decision was made. She and Chet, with help from their older offspring, would build an impoundment to hold water. They would call it Crystal Lake.

The Woodwards set about making something that was, in Iowa in 1896, unusual indeed. Chet, with his team and scraper, boys with shovels and spades doing the hand-work, carved out a depression in the earth that encompassed about an acre. The location was a few yards north of the face of the sandstone bluff, near constantly-flowing springs that were temporarily diverted. The oval-shaped impoundment was eight to ten feet deep on the west end, sloping gradually upward to grade on the east. Alternating his days spent moving earth with planting and tending crops, the job consumed much of the summer. Stacked stone held lake walls in place and sand; fine, wet and heavy sand from the Nishnabotna, was spread on the beach and lake bottom, an overflow stream was created on the west end to carry run-off to the river. A symbolic last step (Chet and Belle would find there was no actual "last step") was to drive a length of four inch pipe deep into a crevice in the bluff. From this pipe water would flow, uninterrupted, summer and winter, through dry years and wet ones, for half a century.

The lake filled and, in the spring of 1897, the Woodwards welcomed guests.

Chapter Three

Captain Huffy's heroism was for naught and the Mary Ann sank.

Crystal Lake, from the very beginning, was much about God, country and patriotism. During the summer it was built, and throughout the first year of operation, newspapers were arousing national sentiments with regard to a revolt going on in Cuba, comparing the struggle there to our own war for independence. In February of 1898 the battleship Maine exploded in Havana harbor, killing 266 American servicemen. One of them, Ensign Darwin Merritt, was from southwest Iowa. Although it was never established that Spain was responsible, neither was it proven she wasn't. Biased newspapers were quick to place the blame. Young men rushed to join the National Guard, the Rough Riders, the navy, anxious to avenge the Maine and Ensign Merritt and run Spain out of Cuba.

War was declared before Crystal Lake opened for the second season. Spain threw in the towel before the season ended. Teddy Roosevelt called it "a splendid little war." For him it was. Others didn't quite understand what the annexation of Hawaii, the seizing of Guam, Manila, and the jungle war in the Philippines had to do with Cuba, but if one took longer than the other both were won. Patriotism reigned.

At Crystal Lake the flag was prominently displayed. When bands played listeners could count on "Yankee Doodle." A song was written, and probably played at the lake, about the USS Maine. "When Johnnie Comes Marching Home Again," which became popular during the Civil War, was revived during the Spanish-American. The year the park opened was the year John Phillip Sousa wrote "Stars and Stripes Forever." This favorite, along with other Sousa creations, would boom out at Crystal Lake during three wars and at regular intervals in between.

While no record exists of the order in which they came, to the lake was added a water slide with a mechanical lift that took a toboggan to the top, a diving board and bath house. A platform for musicians and speakers was erected, picnic areas were designated, flowers planted. A roofed enclosure called 'the pavilion' was built, a structure five or six times longer than it was wide, providing a place for vendors and a shaded seating area for diners and mothers watching children at play. The baseball diamond was laid out, a roller skating rink built, the 102-step stairway near the pavilion was erected. So many came by horse and buggy a barn with stables was added. This was not enough. Another barn was built. Within a year or two of opening the Woodwards decided a larger lake was needed.

Chet, with his team of horses and family labor, went to work again. Called ""Big Lake" at times and "Riverside Lake" at others, located northwest of Crystal Lake and only a few yards east of the river, one goal was an expanse of water large enough to offer steamboat rides. An ill-fated adventure on a sort-of steamboat would mark the grand opening.

Riverside Lake, when completed, consisted of between five and six surface acres of water, none of it very deep. The steamboat it floated was hardly comparable to the paddle-wheel multi-decked craft Jehu, Jane and children came to Iowa on, but it was propelled by steam and it was a boat. It also floated—at least for a while.

The craft consisted of two flat-bottomed rafts, each about eight feet long and sixteen feet wide. These were lashed together, sills put in place and covered with floorboards. A row of seats lined the perimeters.

Mary Jane Ward remembered the day. "Jennie," as she was called, was then a teen-ager. Born in 1885 she grew up in Lewis, never married, had various occupations that included assessor, teacher, librarian, and city clerk. She wrote extensively about memories of her life and times, including the short voyage of the *Mary Ann*.

According to Ward's account, a Lewis businessman named Jake Baker (the same merchant/grocer who was accused of converting used fire hose into bologna casings) owned a steam engine. He loaned it and his services to the occasion. A shallow-water paddle-wheel was devised, and the *Mary Ann* was ready for her maiden voyage. On the appointed day a large crowd gathered. Henry Huffy, captain-for-a-day, took the helm while Chief Engineer Jake Baker managed the mechanics. The Lewis band was brought on board and the remaining space sold to passengers—mostly children—who paid ten cents for a promised three trips around the lake.

Ward tells us the first two circuits were successful, but apparently all was not well in the concealed space between the floor and hull. Below-water gates that should have been bolted shut were not. The *Mary Ann*, with no one realizing she was taking on water, sailed on. Then a youngster spotted something. He thought it was a fish, and a cry went up. Most everyone on board rushed to that side of the craft. The abrupt change in weight distribution caused the water below deck to slosh the same way. Ward remembers that "Home Sweet Home" was being played by the band—but not for long. With her port side riding much too low the doomed vessel took on water faster than before. Within minutes the deck was swamped. Captain Huffy abandoned the wheel long enough to dash through ankle-deep water and grab his two youngsters, then returned to the helm and participated in a valiant effort to reach shore. Captain Huffy's heroism was for naught, and The *Mary Ann* sank. Fortunately the water was so shallow her passengers, including courageous members of the band, waded ashore. We assume women and children went first.

Big Lake was not a success. It was drained soon thereafter and the public went back to enjoying the original.

Photo taken after toboggan slide was installed.

The ill-fated Mary Ann.

Chapter Four

Constable Bates weighed his options, then bade the lady a good evening.

When Chet and Belle Woodward set about to build an amusement park they did not know what interest the general public would have. While they hoped for the best, they could hardly have anticipated the droves of people that quickly made the park a regular destination. Success was immediate and, for a time, got better each year.

In today's era of 24-hour cable, video and computer games, music on demand, radio, new movie releases every weekend and an array of in-home and in-vehicle entertainment systems, we find it difficult to grasp just what Crystal Lake meant.

If people wanted to go to a park there were plenty to choose from. City parks, however, were usually located downtown, under the watchful eyes of city fathers, merchants, the minister and his wife.

Crystal Lake was a mile from town, offered entertainment options not available in any single area park. The Woodwards touted it as being a place for the whole family, and it was. But it was also unrestrained by city ordinances. And it offered a lake—something no other park in the area had.

An expanse of water is visibly appealing. Splashing in shallow water is amusing. A Lewis physician, Dr. Campbell, was among those who proclaimed Crystal Lake's spring water to be good for the body.

Some of those bodies spring-water was good for belonged to girls; girls young and shapely who paraded the beaches in bathing wear that, particularly when soaking wet, offered some slight clue as to form beneath. Boys gawked. Women, dressed in a manner that revealed no skin other than hands and faces, sat in the shade of the pavilion and fretted over the fate of the younger generation.

The lake, during those first years, was advertised as being an ideal place to take a bath. We, who shower after getting out of the swimming pool (knowing what children do in swimming pools), might question the quality of a lake bath. But cleanliness is relative and taking a bath was, for most people, considerably more difficult in the 1890s than it is now. Few farm homes had indoor plumbing, and neither did many in towns. Taking a bath meant going to the well, pumping water, heating it on the cook stove, pouring warm water into a bowl, then using a washcloth to dab away at the places most in need. For special occasions one might heat enough water to put in a small tub, set on a chair with feet submerged, and work from the bottom up. Men could spend a dime at the barber shop and use a tub big enough to sit in, but ladies did not go to barber shops. Come bath day a mother with several children had a choice. The choice was often Crystal Lake. There was, after all, a constant turnover of water. While kids getting out may not have been squeaky, they were a whole lot cleaner than when they got in.

The spring water flowing from the steel pipe tasted good—straight or mixed with other ingredients. Federal prohibition was enacted in 1919. The federal law was not a new concept. Many states had enacted prohibitory laws decades before. Iowa was one of them. This meant when national prohibition became the law of the land folks in our state had a twenty year head start on circumventing it. Liquor could be found by anyone who had the desire. Local law enforcement tended to look the other way as long as the offender was discrete and not being a bother. They could hardly, however, allow a picnicker to consume an illegal substance in a city park. Men who would not consider taking a bottle into the downtown park were less reluctant at the lake. Their tent at this park was, after all, as private as their own home. Drinking was not encouraged at Crystal Lake; certainly not by Chet or Belle Woodward. Still, it was a mile from town and enforcement relied on either a part-time constable or a sheriff from Atlantic. Neither were overly zealous.

Several hundred spectators would come to watch a baseball game, that many to spend an afternoon on the water. Some went to the nearby "Riffles," a shady and normally placid stretch of the Nishnabota. Rowboats were offered for rent. There was, it was said, no better place for a young man to spend an afternoon or evening with a lady.

People flocked to the park for a plethora of reasons—some just to watch others. Nothing, it has been said, draws a crowd like people.

There was never an admission charge. The main entrance was near the present location, off the Jesters Quarry road, which borders the park on the east, with a second driveway to the upper level from the south. To effectively charge an entry fee meant a fence and gates and if the Woodwards ever considered doing this we find no mention of it. They seem to have built the lake and park as much for their own amusement as that of others, having little expectation of financial gain.

They were soon playing the role of host and hostess. Many old photographs, pictures taken of Crystal Lake events with a box camera on a tripod, show us a 4th of July crowd or Old Settler's reunion or similar celebration and we notice a couple in the foreground, or perhaps standing to the side. They are next to each other, smiling, nicely dressed in black even when the weather was warm. Belle and Chet must have enjoyed their role.

She made and sold ice cream. Whether Belle's ice cream was special or the setting just made it seem so, the results were the same. For a generation of youngsters a trip to the lake was not a real trip to the lake without Belle's ice cream. One account has the Woodward children selling lemonade. An ice house was built east of the lake, near the narrow road that went to the upper campgrounds. Crystal Lake ice, cut when it was a foot thick, sold for a premium. It was, after all, the purest of spring water. Dr. Campbell said so.

Dr. Campbell had reason. Water filtered through massive amounts of sandstone undergoes a purification process. It also absorbs essential minerals. An article in the Lewis Standard, as well as Pauline Franklin in her 1976 historical sketch of Lewis, refer to Crystal Lake's "living water."

At the time no one knew just how much water flowed from the springs. Later, in the early 1940s, a representative of the state made some calculations. Chet and Belle always felt there was plenty and gave it away to anyone, even those with containers to take home. We expect they would, however, have been surprised to learn the output was about 30,000 gallons a day.

While the place had a seasonal and semi-official opening and closing date, these were the times during which concessions were sold, bath houses open and, for special events, a lifeguard and keepers of the peace on duty. In reality Crystal Lake never entirely closed. It was private property treated as public. Winter sledding was popular. Ice skating on the lake wasn't satisfying—it was too small, ice often cut from it anyway, and springs that flowed even in sub-zero temperatures created a surface rough and uneven. Riverside Lake was bigger and smoother, but lasted only a few months. That left the Nishnabotna, and it was good. Skaters could embark at Lewis, skate a serpentine mile and a half to the Riffles, and build a bonfire. If the pavilion was boarded up for the winter there was still shelter and a place to sit and talk and warm one's hands around a cup of tea or cocoa before taking another turn on the ice. While the park was not used as much during the off-season it was a year-around destination. Chet and Belle could watch from their home north of the lake, welcoming people to use the land as if it were their own.

Big events—Chautauqua, Veteran's reunions and Old Settlers Day, meant big crowds—six thousand, eight thousand, ten thousand and perhaps more. While newspapers tend to overstate attendance figures, the numbers remain impressive. Crowds this size created matters to be dealt with. Lifeguards and constables were on duty. One of the former was, in 1904, a teenager named Bert Upson.

Elbert Clayton Upson was born on a farm just west of Lewis in 1887. He married Myrtle Carson. He was one of those people, common in his day, who did a lot of things part time rather than one full time. Censuses listed him as a day laborer. He owned a house in Lewis, was a neighbor of J. Frank Berry. As time passed he was offered other work at the lake and accepted. He would joke, in later years, about how he struggled with the task of trying to wash sand out of the bulky rental bathing suits. An even bigger headache came from the long black stockings, an essential part of bathing attire. Young ladies, of various sizes and shapes, tended to be fussy about a proper fit. Stockings did not go with suits. Girls had legs of various girth and length; stockings were made accordingly. At the end of the day girls tended to throw their rented clothing in a heap. Bert and Myrtie were quick to the pile, snatching pairs of soggy stockings before they mingled with others. Failure to do so left them with the tedious task of hanging dozens of stockings from a clothes line and picking through them for matches.

Another job was to deal with parking. Upson's years spanned the transition from horse-power to gasoline engines. Horses and clattering, backfiring automobiles did not get along well. Both had to be parked. Upson had more adventures in this regard than he did as a lifeguard. Attendees were encouraged, if they were able to do so, to either walk from Lewis or take a hack. Better yet, ride the train south of Lewis and stroll to the lake on a pleasant corridor created by the vagaries of the Nishnabotna.

The East Nishnabotna now runs a comparatively straight route through Cass County, bearing south and west toward an eventual juncture with the West Nishnabotna. Before a series of straightening projects, which started in the late 1920s, the river originated and ended in the same locations. What was between, however, was considerably different.

As a boy I once sat in Louie's barber shop and listened to someone describe the East Nishnabotna as it had been. He called it a plate of spaghetti, continued to say if a man and a team had gone to the south end of it, hitched on and pulled the river straight, it would have emptied directly into the Gulf of Mexico. My memory is that the story was told by Bert Upson, but I'm not sure. In any case, this exaggerated depiction of the Nishnabota contained a bit of truth. Old maps show us how the river snaked south after brushing past Lewis, then made a sharp turn to the east as if drawn to the cold springs and bluffs a mile out of the way. The river approached the springs, changed course again, making a loop and turning back from whence it came. Near the top of this elongated horseshoe was a shallow, rock-bottomed stretch that comprised a natural crossing known as "The Riffles."

Those traveling by train to Crystal Lake bought a ticket to Lewis. Trains from the north had no option but to continue on south at least as far as Griswold, where the roundhouse was located.

Dellabelle "Deb" Herbert remembers the train, the roundhouse, passengers getting off the train to help push several tons of locomotive around the rotating tracks, changing direction from south to north. Her parents were regulars at Crystal Lake. Deb remembers the ice cream, the bath houses, the out houses and the baggy grey rental bathing suits that, in her mind, left much to be desired. She camped for a week as a girl scout. She often climbed the 102 steps, pausing on one occasion to carve her initials.

Ms. Herbert, born in 1919, is an Atlantic resident who has experienced and explored local history. She has stories galore. One involves her grandfather, Cyrus Bristol Osborne. Osborne, a cabinet-maker, lived in Lewis in the late 1800s. He made furniture and coffins. He was also an undertaker. One evening he was summoned to the country to pick up a corpse. This he did with his team and wagon. The deceased was put on board. As Osborne started back to town rain was falling. The road was rough and slippery, the horses picking their way in the dark, lunging at times to free a wagon close to miring down. Cyrus and his team arrived in Lewis but the body did not. Somewhere along the way the guest of honor had bounced out. Mr. Osborne was forced back to the muddy, nighttime road and, when the missing was found, to wrestle a slippery and uncooperative passenger into the wagon.

Lady bathers are wearing the rental suits and black stockings that Bert Upson told stories about.

If the train Deb Herbert rode had a genial conductor, and most of them did, passengers for Crystal Lake were dropped off at an unscheduled stop where tracks passed near the open end of the Nishnabotna horseshoe. The walk, with the river on both the right and left, was about the same distance as taking the road from town. The stroll was however, scenic, more pleasant, and usually cleaner. The Lewis lake road was not graveled until the late 1930s. Busy days raised a lot of dust.

By 1901 Jim Myers, a brother of Belle Myers Woodward, was advertising that his hack, drawn by a matched team of stylish mares, would make a run to the lake and back every evening after supper during the summer season. Myers was also available to make the trip at other times upon request. Another hack was operated by Jim Painter, son of a prominent Lewis farmer and investor. Painter, as a boy, had contracted polio. He survived, but for the rest of his life his legs were useless. He made his living driving a team. A family member would harness Painter's horses, carry him to the buggy, and there he spent his days and evenings, making countless trips to Crystal Lake and back.

In 1901 the Old Settler's Association met at Crystal Lake. Tales were told of the good old days. These stories prompted an area newspaper editor to canvas readers for the purpose of determining how many of them, or their parents or grandparents, had migrated to southwest Iowa by covered wagon. The results revealed more about people than about their means of transportation. Despite the fact that settlers came in a trickle before the railroad, in droves after, a surprising number claimed to have made the trip in a covered wagon. More people, the editor of the Villisca Review opined, seemed to have arrived by wagon than had actually arrived.

Following an afternoon program at any of the numerous special events each summer, hundreds of people, sometimes thousands, remained for an evening at lakeside. A so-called "three-picnic-day" was commonplace. Triple picnickers came early, had their hard-boiled eggs and coffee for breakfast, saving sandwiches and fried chicken for dinner and supper. In between were swimming, boating, men pitched horseshoes and women socialized. When the sun went down they danced and roller skated. Men smoked cigars, a few women had cigarettes, and the drinks were not all lemonade. A couple might, from time to time, be seen drifting away from the dance floor to a carriage or grassy hillside.

A man named Bates frequently worked the lake as a keeper of the peace. Constable Bates was the typical officer of his time; there to prevent trouble by his presence, to do his duty without overdoing his duty. At one point during the evening following the Old Settler's reunion of 1901 a female—our newspaper stressed that she was from Atlantic, implying that Lewis ladies would not exhibit such behavior—displayed the effects of overindulgence. She was, through her words and actions, making a spectacle of herself. Constable Bates asked her to either behave or leave the grounds. She let him know she wasn't going to do either and if he tried to make her he'd have a whale of a battle on his hands. Her specific threat, according to the newspaper, was that she'd "paste him in the chops." Constable Bates weighed his options, the news account tells us, then bade the lady a pleasant evening. He drifted off to keep the peace elsewhere.

In the spring of 1903 a young Nebraskan, recently hired as a reporter by the *Atlantic Semi-Weekly Telegraph*, over-exercised his journalistic elegance. The following quaint and flowering depiction appeared in that paper's May 12th edition.

The writer indulged in a little solitaire excursion to the summer-time home of the far-famed and easily accessible Crystal Lake on Friday morning. Never before have we had the pleasure of aiming our optics at the place, and this early-in-the-season sight-seeing jaunt was made in order that we could begin to comprehend the grandeur of things before the season opening sometime next month. We want to get used to things gradually, hence we did not attempt to see all there is to be seen this time of year. The site of the lake is only a half-hours walk from the city of Lewis if you start in the proper direction. For the native of this section the place holds little attraction because he has seen it in all its dazzlingness during the diving season. But to those who hail from the wind-swept prairies of Nebraska where a watering place is unknown everything here is serenely lovely. When the projectors of this miniature Newport decided upon the site they did so with their artistic dip-needles in proper shape, for there is no finer site for a lake in this part of Iowa. It really does seem that the hills and bluffs were built about the lake instead of the lake being brought to the hills. Of course the lake doesn't resemble a watering place as much now as it will when the leak-hole in the side of the shore closest the river is plugged up so the water coming from the springs in the hill will flood the lake-site. It takes only about three weeks to run the banks full enough for the toboggan slider to work properly. Ample shade is provided by giant trees and by the perpendicular hills that bathe their heads in the altitudinous blue. Johnny-Jump-Ups and wild roses abound in profusion to please the lover of nature's art, and in the dim distance can be heard the tinkling of a cow-bell which sends its music upon the wafting Zephyrs every time the spotted cow called Speck drags her nose along a few inches to get a bigger mouthful of grass. The home of the lizard, squirming things, and chiggers is not here. Instead twittering songbirds cleave to and fro through the sunshine with paeans of praise welling from their worm-stained bills. The breezes steal and rustle through the trees and seem to again whisper some of the tales of love which were in days a-gone breathed into shell-like ears that before the season closed got so badly sunburned they needed a lotion. While gazing upon the natural beauty here one's mind turns to the old yet beautiful legend that the first maiden who inserted her pearly whiteness into the lake at the opening of the season would be a bride before the New Year. The patter of a few raindrops upon the pavilion roof comes like a faint echo of the rhythmic tread of young people who have floated about through perfumed air and ecstasy to some soul-stirring waltz played on a two-bit Jews harp. One could, he feels, linger in this fairy paradise forever, his very being imbued with peaceful, restful joy which no mortal tongue could describe were it not for the fact that a hungry toad jumps upon his hand in an attempt to snare a mosquito and reminds the dreamer that he'll have to mosey homeward if he expects to get his dinner.

A few weeks later the same paper reported that H.K. Myers (probably Harry, also known as Henry, a nephew of Belle Woodward) was in Council Bluffs on a matter having to do with a bowling alley he'd be installing at Crystal Lake in the near future. This plan apparently fell through, as we find no further mention of a bowling alley.

Crowds kept coming. On July 13, 1905, The Atlantic Messenger announced that special passenger trains would run for the annual Old Settlers Day at Crystal Lake, with bargain fares being given in Atlantic, Wiota, Audubon, Anita and Griswold. Hacks would be at the Lewis depot in abundance. The following year the August 30th edition of the *Cass County Democrat* carried five separate items on Crystal Lake: The Congregational picnic was held there, on Sunday a large number of visitors from Carson were on a week-long camping outing, about 120 members of the Odd Fellows convened at the lake for social purposes, a group from the Lewis Christian Church picnicked there, and a dance would be held the following Saturday at the skating rink.

That summer Red Oak's National Guard unit marched to Atlantic as part of their annual training. Leading the way was First Sergeant Owen

Hawkins. Hawkins had endeared himself to his men during eighteen months of fighting in the Philippines. Years later, for World War l, he would again volunteer. On a September day in 1918, during a fierce engagement during the St. Mihiel offensive, Company M was badly shot up and pinned down. At the advanced age of 44, Sgt. Hawkins "took care of his boys," making a solo raid that resulted in the nullification of a machine gun and the capture of 17 German soldiers. For this he was awarded the French Croix De Guerre and the Distinguished Service Cross.

Hawkins had the good judgment, on that training foray in 1905, to "take care of his boys" by spending a day and night in bivouac at Crystal Lake.

Mr. and Mrs. Frank Conrad of Griswold were managers in '06, the first year since opening that Belle and Chet Woodward relinquished that responsibility.

It is difficult to find an issue of any Atlantic, Griswold or Lewis newspaper published during the summer months of that era that does not contain one or more articles on Crystal Lake. Not all were positive. In early October of 1906 Chet Woodward had the Conrads close down in order to help him with corn picking. A group of young people drove up from Griswold, found the pavilion not open for business, and registered their indignation with a written complaint that made the front page of the *Telegraph*. How dare they?

The July 15, 1907 *Democrat* carried a front page feature on the previous Sunday's baseball game between Lewis and Exira. A special train ran from Audubon carrying five passenger coaches, all filled. Paid admission was nearly 1,000. Dozens of additional spectators cheated, watching from the road or other vantage point. Lewis, in part because of a final-inning error by the first basemen, blew a lead and lost the game. A second news item had to do with Frank Lumsden of Atlantic, who was driving his automobile toward the lake. Coming from there was a horse-drawn carriage driven by Mrs. Rosa Smiley of Lewis. With her were two young daughters of Mr. and Mrs. Levi Disbrow. Lumsden made a sharp turn in front of team, frightening them. During the runaway Mrs. Smiley and the girls were thrown out. The latter two were not injured, but Mrs. Smiley suffered a number of contusions and severe bruises. The story of the baseball game was above the fold—the accident below.

In the spring of '07 a newspaper called *The Farmer's Messenger* announced that Chet Woodward would again manage the park. A chap named Perry Showers would run the restaurant, promising plenty of good food regardless of the size of the crowds.

The fall of '08 brought a new experience. Two Baptist preachers, Rev. Broadfoot and Rev. Charles, brought nine converts to Crystal Lake and baptized them by immersion. (*Telegraph*, 9-11-08)

On August 9, 1911, the *Messenger* told of several horse-drawn cabs meeting at Sunnyside Park in Atlantic to transport all Atlantic Methodist Sunday School classes to the annual Methodist picnic at Cold Springs. The event, attended by members of Methodist Sunday Schools throughout Cass County, drew several hundred children.

The *Atlantic News Telegraph* said the streets of Atlantic looked like "the famous deserted city" on July 4, 1913. The front page article continued:

The largest crowd from here went to Lewis, where the Crystal Lake resort did the biggest business in its history. Autos and buggies carrying people there lined the roads all day and the resort itself was a mass of people, buggies and automobiles. The resort folks reaped a harvest and an idea of the business done can be gained when it is known that the refreshment pavilion at Crystal Lake used 175 cases of pop from the Atlantic Bottling Works and was out of that refreshment before the day was even nearly over. The bathing pool in the lake did a big business, the merry go round was busy and the skating rink a lively place until late at night. At the airdome the picture show drew a large number of people. The crowd at the baseball game between the Atlantic Merchant's Greys and Griswold team was immense, with gate receipts being over $231. Picnic parties thronged the woods and the automobiles which bore the people there flew pennants of Stuart, Casey, Dexter, Avoca and many other places farther away. The employees at Crystal Lake were a tired lot when night came.

The following year brought comparable crowds, but also an unfortunate accident. Elmer Todd, a 53-year-old hired man of a Lewis area farmer named Fred Switzer, was among several thousand revelers. On a mid-summer night, shortly after darkness, he was seated on the grass along the road behind some parked cars, one of which was owned by Frank Smith of Griswold. Smith started his car, preparing to leave. He backed up. Not seeing Todd, and ran over him. The distraught Smith helped the badly injured Todd into his car and took him to the Lewis

Hospital. There were initial fears that Todd would not live, however a news item on July 6th reported that Todd was then expected to survive, but would likely be partially paralyzed as the result of a broken back.

At Crystal Lake – about 1905

Bandstand in use during a 1905 event.

Crystal Lake was a must for Boy Scouts, Girl Scouts, Campfire Girls and Cub Scouts. Ethyl Berry, in one of the many historical columns she wrote for the Farm Monthly section of the Atlantic News Telegraph, tells of George Voss who, in the late teens and early 1920s, was scoutmaster of the Exira troop. It was his custom, each summer, to lead his boys on a hike from Exira to Crystal Lake. Packing tents, food and other supplies, the boys would set out on a march of just over 25 miles. They'd make the trek in a day, pitch camp and spend a week exploring, swimming, building campfires and cooking over them; studying plants and wildlife, telling stories and dreaming of Indians and the days when elk and buffalo watered at the springs. At the end of a week the scouts would pack up and make the twenty-five mile hike back to Exira.

Chapter Five

The law was clear as spring water—baseball could not be played in Lewis on Sunday

"Blue laws," ordinances designed to retain the Sabbath and keep it holy, were once common to Iowa towns. These ordinances prohibited or severely restricted commerce and certain other activities on Sunday. Some did not allow any business transactions to take place, including the sale of products, on Sunday. While most towns. including Lewis, modified this stance by allowing the purchase of milk, baby food, medications and certain other necessities, playing frivolous games for entertainment purposes remained forbidden. The offense was doubly egregious if admission was charged.

Lewis ordinance number 19, section 10, was enacted prior to the building of Crystal Lake and continued in effect long after lake diamond had grown to weeds. The law was clear as spring water—baseball could not be played in Lewis on Sunday. (Sunday baseball may still be unlawful. If ordinance 19, section 10, was repealed I found no record of it.)

The Sunday prohibition of athletic contests was not a problem for high school teams. The town teams, however, consisted of working men and, if they were good enough, a few high school boys. Without lights to play at night, with Saturday being an important business day, finding time for games was a problem. While players might assemble on a weeknight evening for practice, getting enough for a game was difficult. This was particularly true for the visitors, who had to round up the team and then travel. Sunday afternoon was ideal, even allowing enough time for a double-header.

Town team baseball, inhibited by blue laws and the lack of facilities outside towns, blossomed in Cass County with the coming of Crystal Lake. The date of the first game played there is unknown, but it was probably within a year or two of opening. From that point on baseball was as much a part of Crystal Lake as swimming and skating.

Newspapers depict the intensity of these contests. When reporters wrote that a game was hard-fought, they meant it. Umpires were generally not the best—sometimes biased, sometimes incompetent—and in either case most were not good at taking control when tempers flared. Fans tended to be rowdy, taunting, and when jeers directed toward players on one team angered fans of the other, a bit of fisticuffs in the stands often followed. Players wore spikes. They did not wear helmets. Gloves were thin, almost without padding. The field was rough, bad bounces part of the game. For forty years the diamond was located near the road on the northeast part of the park. Strangers, unfamiliar with the place, sometimes drove across the outfield.

These amateur players became revered by their fans. Smiley, Porter, Evans, Linke, Anderson, Casady, Kaiser, Sheets, Kirchoff, Sanny, Burnside, Merritt, Krisinger and more. Jim Porter was a player, and a good one in the early 1900s. He taught his son, Dave, to pitch.

In the early 1930s Lila Mundorf Kunze learned to swim at Crystal Lake. She remembers outdoor dances by the pavilion, picnics, roller skating, the flash flood that caused an employee of Mick Quinn to scurry up a tree with a pair of monkeys from Quinn's Zoo. And she recalls her Uncle Jim Porter, her cousin Dave, and baseball.

Several of those interviewed for this book said Dave Porter was the best pitcher they ever saw. I initially assumed they meant the "best from Lewis," or "best at Crystal Lake." Bernice Casady let me know otherwise. Some considered him to be the finest pitcher they ever watched, anywhere, anyplace.

Bernice Kirkhoff Casady was born in 1914. She knew Charley Willey, editor of the Standard, as a man of good humor. She experienced Crystal Lake as a child and saw dozens of baseball games. When Willey began advocating for a state park—a park the state would take only if it was given to them—she suited up with other members of the high school band and, on the back of an open truck bed, toured the county playing music and soliciting donations.

She remembers the roller rink, the calliope and Pee Wee Ingram renting skates. Like everyone who frequented the place she was impressed by the water, remembers two steel pipes from which it flowed. She remembers the effect of baseball on her wedding.

Bernice began dating Claud Casady in high school. They planned to marry, but the Depression was tough and Claud wanted to work, to save a little money. The ceremony finally took place in 1937; six years after Bernice graduated.

In a day when hardly a boy reached 8th grade without a nickname, Claud Casady was "Dutch." A good many boys in the generation that followed his became customers at his Standard Oil station, knew him for years, yet had no idea that "Dutch" was not his given name. Casady was, in the 1930s, one of the town team's better players. So was "Pete" Kirkhoff, Bernice's brother.

Bernice and Dutch planned their marriage for Sunday, September 5th. As the date approached, the Merchants entered a Labor Day weekend tournament in Macedonia. Bernice's brother had a decision. He chose baseball and missed the wedding. Claud could hardly do likewise. There would be no honeymoon trip, however, because Lewis won and played again the following day. Mr. Dutch Casady started. His bride watched.

"Dave Porter," Bernice Casady states with the firm conviction of a 97-year-old woman who is entirely sure of herself, "could throw a baseball 100 miles an hour." Porter was a tall, slender, long-armed youngster who not only threw hard he could, even in high school, hit a target. In many of his games his target was the glove of Pete Kirkhoff.

A catcher's mitt then was not the ergonomically designed mass of space-age foam it is today. There was little to protect a catcher's hand. "Every time Pete caught while Dave Porter was pitching he put a piece of beef steak in his glove," Casady said, "and by the time the game was over it wasn't much more than hamburger."

She tells of major league scouts who trekked to Lewis to see this high school phenomenon. Porter was all but certain to land a major league contract, but in his senior year something went wrong.

Bernice Casady tells of a high school tournament, probably the annual county competition. Porter pitched the first game, going all the way in a contest Lewis won handily. He was asked to pitch again the next day and he did. Somewhere during the late innings his arm began to hurt. He kept pitching, but it wasn't the same. Porter assumed a couple of days off would be the cure. It wasn't. He pitched for the town team, and against that level of competition a 90 mph fastball is as baffling as one of 100. But he was not as fast as he had been and major league scouts lost interest. "He felt terrible about that."

Mrs. Casady, seated in her room at 800 Chestnut, described a young man who truly believed he could have been a big-time major league pitcher, the bitter disappointment he felt for years over what might have been.

She speaks of another disappointment. "Those people raised money. We helped. Claud and I contributed. The state took the park because it was given to them, then they tore down everything there was to love about it. What they did was a disgrace. I wouldn't let my kids swim there."

Bernice McGaffin Burnside, born the same year as Mrs. Casady, now resides at Heritage House in Atlantic. She smiles at the mention of Pete Kirkhoff slipping a steak into his glove. "Eldon did the same thing." The man she would marry, Eldon Burnside, caught Porter in high school.

Mrs. Burnside remembers the fund-raiser, thinks she and her husband gave about $10 at a time when $10 was a lot of money. She speaks of the clear, cold water, the sand bottom and beach, the stone walls of Crystal Lake. She's a witty and imaginative lady—has written poetry that would bring tears to a stone. She seemed close to laughter when she remembered Quinn's Zoo. "Mick Quinn, while he was manager, brought in all manner of entertainment. For two or three years he had that sideshow we called 'Quinn's Zoo.' Except for a couple of monkeys it was nothing but animals we have around here—raccoons, a squirrel—the sort of thing you'd see any day. He had them in cages in the grove of shade trees east of the pavilion."

Bernice Burnside knew Crystal Lake and she knows baseball. Bob Smiley, who married her younger sister, was a pitcher of note. Lewis relished beating Lyman, and Cumberland and Wiota and Atlantic and especially Griswold. And of course the Griswold team was among those that wanted nothing more than to thump Lewis.

In the early 1920s a Lewis boy named Calburt "Cab" Marker played the game. He loved baseball, was probably better at football. When

Marker, born in 1905, died at the age of 82 his obituary referred to him as a "sports enthusiast." This is a sizeable understatement. He played every high school sport available, then began organizing and managing. He was a high school sports icon, in one way or another, for nearly seventy years. Marker umpired, refereed, kept score, sold tickets. He was a fixture at the scorer's table for Lewis basketball games from the late 1920s until the school burned. Then he followed the team to Griswold.

Marker went into partnership with his father in a Lewis hardware store in 1925. At the same time Marker, who had just turned twenty, took over as manager of the Lewis town baseball team. They'd been given a lot of names in the past. Marker called them the "Merchants." His teams were "semi-pro," so called because some out-of-town talent was given a few dollars to play, others got a cut of the gate.

Marker brought a degree of civility to Crystal Lake baseball. Articles printed after he took charge refer to contests being "clean" and "fair" and conducted with" good sportsmanship."

Lewis teams under Marker were good; good enough to take on teams made up of players from packing plants and breweries in Omaha and Des Moines and hold their own. Betty McGaffin Sanny (her husband, Hank, was a regular infielder), recalls Lewis facing a team that featured Satchell Page. Marker did not rely entirely on Lewis residents. Home-town fans wanted to pull for home-town boys, but they also wanted to win. When Marker could get them the King brothers from Atlantic, players good enough to play professionally, were on the Lewis squad.

Baseball then was segregated. When the Griswold American carried an article saying that Lewis would be playing "a fast colored team from Kansas City" we can be assured the team was entirely black. White teams were all white. Cab Marker must have raised eyebrows when, in the late 1930s, he began using a black man, Bill Sweets of Lewis, as a pinch runner. We find no record of Sweets ever playing a position, or batting, and have no way of knowing if he had a talent for either. But he was a speedy runner and Cab Marker put him on the team, in a Lewis Merchants uniform, and sent him in to play.

While we may never know with certainty, there is reason to believe one of the best right-handers in baseball history, Hall-of-Famer Bob Feller, pitched a game at Crystal Lake.

Dick Marshall graduated from Lewis High School in 1953. He and his brother, Lee, were Cleveland Indian fans at a time when the Indians were World Series contenders. Their star pitcher was Feller, who was born in Van Meter, Iowa.

Following his high school and college years, long after Feller had retired, Dick's work required extensive travel. He recalls a day in the early 1990s when inclement weather caused lengthy flight delays at Washington's Reagan National Airport. The Northwest Airlines gate area was packed with travelers, many having waited for hours. With little to pass the time but an already-read newspaper, Dick took note of a man across the room—a man who looked very much like Bob Feller. Dick approached, introduced himself, told the man he thought he recognized him. Feller smiled, gave a fictitious name. Dick apologized and returned to his seat. Shortly thereafter Feller had a change of heart. He acknowledged who he was and he and Marshall engaged in a genial conversation. Feller asked where Dick Marshall was from. He was told Lewis in southwest Iowa. Feller didn't initially recognize the name, but after a few moments asked if there was a ball diamond by a little lake a short distance south of town. Dick said there was. Feller said he'd pitched there when about 14 or 15 years old.

Feller was born in 1910. The game he was referring to would have taken place in the mid 1920s. Unfortunately, Cass County newspapers did not generally print the names of visiting players. We find reference to a "fast team from Des Moines," and in the mid-20s Lewis occasionally ran into a pitcher who shut them out. One of them may have been Bob Feller, the famed "Heater from Van Meter."

There was no greater fan of Crystal Lake, and baseball, then Charles Willey.

"Charley," as his friends called him, was born in Oskaloosa in 1864. Five years later his family moved to Atlantic, where an older brother became editor of the Atlantic Messenger. By the late 1870s Charles was working as a printer's devil, and there he learned the trade. He also, as a young man in Atlantic, played some baseball. He moved to Des Moines and worked for a printer for a few years, returning to Cass County in 1900 to take a job with J.W.B Fletcher, owner and publisher of The Lewis Standard. As Fletcher grew older Willey expanded his role with the paper, eventually writing most of the articles. In 1919 Charles Willey bought the *Standard*.

Baseball, not allowed in town due to "blue laws," was a natural at Crystal Lake.

Baseball drew Willey to Crystal Lake. Past his playing days, he attended virtually every game as both a fan and reporter. He wrote at length about the marathon game of 1908 in which Lewis rallied late to tie Lyman, then went on to win 5-4 in 14 innings. Twenty-three years later Willey would help organize an old-timer's game, a fund-raiser that was part of his save-the-park effort. Dick Woodward and Jim Porter played in both games. In the 1908 contest Porter struck out 17 batters. He was less impressive in the second, but Willey wrote that Porter still had a pretty good fast ball.

If baseball took Willey to Crystal Lake on Sunday afternoons throughout the summer, other activities had him there even more often. The annual Chautauqua was news, family reunions made the social column, church picnics, the big 1927 log-rolling contest, the announcement in 1928 that park manager Bert Upson had not only acquired new bathing suits for rent, he was making season bathing tickets available for just $2.

The steady flow of campers came to intrigue Willey, and as the future of the lake grew clouded Willey used the campers to advance an idea.

Chapter Six

*Black walnut timber is sure to be of great value
in the construction of aeroplanes*

Within a few years the park became busy to the extent the Woodwards opted for a lease arrangement that would have someone else oversee day-to-day operations. Frank Carr managed in 1908, adding lawn tennis and croquet. The Woodward boys, Jennie Ward writes, took a turn. One was Ed (Charles Edward, born in 1879). Recently married, Ed set up a tent and he and his bride spent a summer living and working at the park. Ed then bought a drug store in Griswold and park management was turned over to Elbert "Bert" and Myrtle "Mertie" Upson.

Suffering from diabetes, Belle died in 1916. Chet, then 71 years old, moved to Lewis. Jennie ward fretted that without Belle's ice cream, and oversight, things would not be the same.

By the late 1920s Charles Willey had a growing concern. Southwest Iowa, and indeed the entire Midwest, is dotted with sites that used to be. Willey was aware of one-time harness tracks and revival sites and fairgrounds that had seen their day and were plowed under. The grand amusement park and swimming pool built by the Tylers of Villisca became, much of it, a cornfield. Closer to Atlantic was Lamb's Lake, five miles north and, in Pymosa Township, was Smith's Lake. According to a *News Telegraph* article from March of 1909, Smith's Lake had a pool with boating and bathing; a baseball diamond and toboggan slide were contemplated, and then the place ceased to be. Rural amusement parks led a tenuous existence—enduring only as long as someone was willing to give them needed attention. Charley Willey fully understood the problem. Chet Woodward was growing old. When he died, unless a change was made beforehand, the farm and Crystal Lake would pass to his heirs. Those with any interest had already tried park management, and moved on.

While Charles Willey did not write about D'ing Darling, did not carry his cartoons, he was well aware of the man and his ideas.

Jay Norwood Darling (1876-1962), a long-time cartoonist for the Des Moines Register, won two Pulitzer Prizes. He was decidedly Republican and conservative in his politics, a friend of Herbert Hoover, yet he forged an alliance with FDR and other liberal Democrats in order to advance his cause.

The name ' D'ing,' a contraction of his last name, was a remnant of college days that he would retain throughout his remarkable career. While Darling favored conservation of all natural resources, his focus was waterfowl and the wetlands migratory birds needed to flourish. He had a receptive audience. Regardless of political persuasion, few people could contemplate the total elimination of the passenger pigeon, which Darling often reminded them of, and disregard his repeated warnings that more species were poised to vanish. His cartoons were front and center in the biggest newspaper in Iowa, syndication made them available to dozens of other publications. He was exceptionally good at his craft. His drawings were quality—he designed the first Federal duck stamp—and his message was clear and forceful, yet delivered with good taste and humor.

Conservationists, bird-watchers, hunters, fishermen; all climbed on the Darling bandwagon. And, in part because they did, politicians followed.

In the mid 1920s, as Willey was contemplating the future of Crystal Lake, Darling began advocating for a "25 year plan" for the preservation and creation of wetlands and the expansion of Iowa's system of state parks.

The movement did not start with Darling. Those like Chet and Belle Woodward, who came to Iowa as children in the 1850s and 60s, were senior citizens in the early years of the 20th century. They had witnessed a plethora of changes. A growing number of these people realized not everything that changes is for the better. Regrets were few over the passage of Indians, bear and bison, but prairie chickens were all but gone, as were deer and elk and otters and wild turkeys. Precious little virgin prairie remained. Forests had been cut, wetlands drained, and what virgin land remained was shrinking year-by-year.

As people age their appreciation for what once was tends to increase. What once was, in much of Iowa, was all but gone. Preserving key areas that remained was discussed by voters and elected officials. In 1918, with World War l in progress, patriotism and love of country running high, the 37th Iowa General Assembly acted on behalf of conservation in several ways. Fearing the extinction of certain species, citing the passenger pigeon, they banned the hunting of mourning doves. The legislature also created two state agencies; one with enforcement authority of fish and game laws under a State Fish and Game Warden, the other the State Board of Conservation.

Section 1 of the bill gave the State Board of Conservation, with supervision by the Executive Council, authority to "establish public parks in any county of the State, upon the shores of lakes, streams or other waters of the state, or at any other places which have, by reason of their location become historic or which are of scientific interest, or by reason of their natural scenic beauty or location be adapted therefore, and the said Board of Conservation, under the supervision of said Executive Council, is hereby authorized to improve and beautify such parks." The bill went on to give condemnation power, authorize the erection of dams, and other details necessary to allow the board to go about their mission. The State Game Warden was directed to establish, through the administrative rule process, a fee schedule for hunting and fishing licenses. While a portion of this revenue would be retained by the warden to cover expenses of his office, the remainder was to go to the State Board of Conservation for use in establishing, improving and maintaining state parks.

The portion of the bill setting forth science, historic value and natural and scenic beauty as being criteria for state parks would be much discussed by Willey and his Crystal Lake/state park proponents.

The first members of the four-person Board of Conservation were L.H. Pammel of Ames, J.F. Ford of Fort Dodge, Joseph Kelso of Bellevue and E.R. Harlan of Des Moines. Pammel was a professor of botany at Iowa

State University, Harlan the curator of the State Historical Department.

Among the first things they did as a group was make a tour of the state evaluating various sites as potential "Memorial State Parks" (so designated to honor those who served in the recently ended war). Their report was prepared in hard-cover book format and a copy sent to each of Iowa's public libraries. The book has some oddities. It was probably printed by the state printing office, but there is not a page so indicating. The date of publication is unclear. Stamped on the cover is the date "1919." The book, however, refers to several state parks that were acquired after 1919. Perhaps the book was originally printed that year, followed by an amended version after the acquisition of additional parks.

What is certain is that in 1918-19 the four board members had several meetings and visited all corners of Iowa. They express excitement about a number of potential park sites in eastern Iowa, particularly along the Mississippi. They loved the northern lake region. They refer to the northeast as "Little Switzerland." In southwest Iowa, however, they felt it necessary to visit only three counties. The board compiled a list of over 100 sites which were, in their words, "Suggested by Responsible Citizens as Suitable for Public Park Purposes and So Regarded by the Board of Conservation, From Which Selections Will Be Made." Other than a couple of locations near the Missouri river, southwest Iowa does not make the list. In subsequent meetings the board was lobbied extensively. They were asked, and agreed, to take a closer look at Pilot Mound, Twin Lake, Wall Lake, Storm Lake, the so-called largest boulder in the United States in Floyd County. They re-visited Bone Yard Hollow, Ledges in Boone County, Devil's Backbone, steamboat Rock, Wild Cat Den, Red Rock, Keosauqua, Ottumwa and adjacent regions, Odessa Lake, Muscatine County, northeastern Iowa, Jackson County, Bixby's Park and so on. Their trip to southwest Iowa was brief. The closest they came to Cass County was Montgomery, of which they wrote: "like others in southwest Iowa, it has little to offer . . . " They felt a few roadside parks would be adequate. The board was impressed, however, by native walnut trees that grew in the valley of the Nishnabotna. The state, they opined, might do well to buy some of this cheap land populated with these trees as "black walnut timber is sure to be of great value in the future for the construction of aeroplanes." At the time airplanes had wooden propellers and there were those who thought walnut was ideal for this purpose.

The board established priorities during these trips and meetings. They also solicited publicly for donations, discussed ways to encourage citizens and communities to contribute monetarily, and to give desirable sites to the state.

In July of 1919 two well-to-do spinster sisters from Muscatine County, Miss Emma Brant and Miss Clara Brandt, offered the board about 60 acres that would become Wild Cat Den State Park State Park. Their experience is of interest as it parallels what would take place a few years later with Crystal Lake. Noteworthy in the Brandt transaction are the conditions agreed to; conditions that include a requirement that the board proceed within two years to make specific improvements, to provide a custodian and acquire additional land. If these detailed conditions were not met within two years the property would revert to the previous owners. Another condition the board agreed to was to "maintain forever the area as a state park."

The board went about their work in those early years, work that included preparing appropriation bills for proposed parks and improvements. Lake Manawa near Council Bluffs was on their list, but that was about it for this part of the state. In the entire 328 page book Cass County is not mentioned.

There probably weren't many southwest Iowans who read the book. Those who did had reason to feel slighted. The board felt it appropriate to give higher priority to scenic formations and landscapes in parts of the state that were, in their view, more striking. An issue, though, was that their appropriation requests were drawn from the general fund. Southwest Iowans were paying the same tax rate as those in the north and east. They were helping pay for parks 200 or 300 miles away, just as they had been roads, and as time passed the resentment grew.

Ironic it is that at the same time the conservation movement was gaining traction, as Darling's call for wetlands and marshes found an increasingly receptive audience, tax money was being spent to straighten rivers. The straightening of the Nishnabota south of Lewis meant an end to the "Horsehoe Walk" from the railroad's unofficial drop-off point. The "Riffles" ceased to be. Romantic boat rides from the amusement park—rides on the placid water of a slow-moving river with overhanging trees that offered shady, secluded nooks for those special moments— became a thing of the past.

Betty McGaffin Sanny says there was more to it than that. "There weren't many people around here who thought straightening the rivers was a good idea." Sanny, born a half mile northeast of Lewis in 1918, was too young to have waded the "Riffles." She was, however, old enough to hear her father and others talk about the folly of trying to make a river run where it doesn't want to. "They believed a river was where it was for a reason. Straightening it would drain water faster, but the river would try to go back to where it belonged." This, locals predicted, was sure to cause serious erosion and never-ending problems because the river would, every time high water came, cut away banks seeking to get back to where nature intended.

I asked Matt Dolllison, a biologist for the Natural Resources Conservation Service, if he had an opinion on this. His answer surprised me.

"Those people," he said, "were exactly right." With that he turned to a computer screen and scrolled through a series of slides—photographs and drawings—showing the negative, long-term effect of river straightening. Through aerial photos from the 1930s and government survey maps dating to about 1840 we traced a small portion of the course of Deep Creek and the East Nishnabotna, then overlaid a current map. The effect was startling. I envisioned the straightening project we know as the Rock Cut as eliminating a long, looping curve called the horseshoe bend. The horseshoe, at the time Crystal Lake was built, bore scant resemblance to a horseshoe. To call it a loop or bend is to overlook the fact that it consisted of dozens of bends, small ones, one after another. To walk from Lewis to Crystal Lake was perhaps a mile. To follow the river to the same destination was a much greater distance.

Dollison then scrolled out and we viewed the maps from a wider scale, seeing the river as it entered and left Cass County. The Horseshoe was a series of small horseshoes. Upson's depiction of the river as a plate of spaghetti was a good one.

Chapter Seven

He was sick and he was going blind

We don't know exactly when Charles Willey seized the idea of Crystal Lake becoming a state park. He first began making hints in his paper in 1930. Willey, from the time he moved to Lewis and watched Crystal Lake baseball, was a lover of the park. In the early 1920s he started carrying a weekly front page note during the summer season about campers at the lake. He was impressed, felt there to be an untapped potential—although he doesn't use the word—in tourism. People had been camping near the springs for 10,000 years or more. The building of the lake increased this usage, and then came the automobile. Previously campers had been mostly local—now many were from other states, both coasts, a fact that Willey felt was significant. He was not a Lewis native, but during his thirty years in town it would be difficult to find anyone who did more promoting. Willey observed in his column that travelers could pitch a tent at the lake without a fee. Financial benefit to Lewis merchants came from their purchase of gasoline and groceries. If they found the park pleasant, and many did, they might linger for a day or two. And as Willey stopped to chat with campers he found many returned time and again.

Now, with Chet Woodward's situation in his mind, along with the D'ing Darling inspired call for a state park or lake in every county, Willey saw a solution.

In June of 1931 The Des Moines Register's Sunday edition carried a feature that expressed a sentiment similar to what Willey had been saying for some time. "Motor to an Iowa State Park" was the headline, and below was a drawing and map showing destinations—many of which were not actually state parks. A place of interest in Cass County, according to the article, was "John Brown's Country." A corresponding mark on the map located the home of W.S. Roberts west of Lewis, referring to it as "an Underground Railroad Station." We don't know how the Roberts family, working the farm and living in the house, felt about being a designated tourist destination. They could, of course, direct visitors to nearby Crystal Lake.

Willey reprinted a part of the article, then added his own thoughts.

Nature has done much to supply everything necessary for a state park at Crystal Lake. There is an abundance of shade, a good camp ground and never-ending supply of spring water. Crystal Lake is located only a short distance from the Underground Railroad Station. Less than half a mile north of the station is the marker of the spot where the old Mormon Trail from Keokuk and the one from Des Moines converged. The re-routing of Nr. 32 left this tablet lost in a cornfield. For more than 6 years the Standard has kept a record of the tourists who stopped in our free campground. Many of these people took autos and we prepared a communication to be published in "The Old Home Paper." We believe we are entitled to a state park and hope the State Board of Conservation and the Historical Department will at least come have a look.

Willey had previously written about a possible state park—now, for the first time, he uses the word "entitled." He believes this to be the case, as he will point out in subsequent editorials, in part because Lewis has been repeatedly given what he calls a "raw deal" by the state. The rawest of raw deals, in his mind, had to do with roads.

One road issue that incensed Willey was the re-routing of Highway 32. What he referred to as "Nr. 32" would later be designated, and is now known as, Highway 6. Long before becoming "Nr. 32," before even automobiles, it was a wagon route called "The White Pole Road." When Willey moved to Lewis it was a primary highway (although it was mostly dirt) from river to river. Aside from the railroad, this was the main artery from Des Moines to Council Bluffs and Omaha.

In the 1920s plans were made for changes, including widening, grading and hard-surfacing. Towns along the way had a vital interest in any contemplated changes in location. Today the norm is for major thoroughfares to bypass cities. Then they went through downtown, taking travelers into the business district where merchants wanted them. The White Pole Road went south from Atlantic, past the Lewis cemetery and through town, then continued on west. Representatives of the Iowa Highway Commission met with the Cass County Board of Supervisors to reach an agreement on the specifics of the planned project in this county. Willey and others from Lewis, along with delegations from Wiota and Anita, were in attendance.

This was a matter they felt the need to be fully informed on. According to Willey, assurance was given that any possible changes would be openly discussed and all concerned given an opportunity to express their views. Atlantic, the county seat, was safe. Anita and Wiota and Lewis thought they were as well, being told the road would be paved through Cass County without deviation from the existing course. The Lewis group went home believing the town would only be improved by the paving project.

Somewhere between the meeting in Cass County and the onset of actual construction, the Highway Commission had a change of mind. Willey and Lewis businessmen didn't know until the state acquired land north of town and made plans for building a new bridge. The highway, Willey was stunned to learn, would make the turn to the west nearly a mile short of the cemetery, completely by-passing Lewis. Willey was outraged. We assume business people in Lewis, particularly those catering to motorists, were equally upset.

Without doubt Willey was correct when he charged that a promise on the route had been made, then broken. In the October 20, 1927, edition of the *Atlantic News Telegraph* appears a map released by the Highway Commission showing primary roads that would be paved. Highway Number 32 is clearly shown as running past the cemetery, through Lewis, then west across the county line before jogging north to the present location.

The town's woes with the Highway Commission did not stop there. Many felt the road that did pass through town, connecting what are now highways 71 and 6, was an inadequate appeasement, particularly as the road remained dirt for years.

Willey also put forth a plan for the routing of Highway 48, which was to run from Griswold to 32 (the present Highway 6). Willey had two routes in mind. One would be to run north of Griswold to the existing road that went east to Crystal Lake, past the lake, then north, by the school house and on to Highway 32 (6). Willey's other plan had 48 turning northeast at the northern edge of Griswold, running at a diagonal to the park, thence north. Either, Willey said, made perfect sense. This made Crystal Lake, which if he had his way would soon be a state park, easily accessible from all directions.

Another noteworthy item in Willey's July 9th article is his reference to the Underground Railroad. With talk of state parks in the air a good many historians, including members of the state Historical Association, saw an opportunity to further their agenda. The statute included historic value as a factor to be considered in choosing park sites. The director of the Iowa Historical Department was a member of the Board of Conservation. Willey repeatedly pushed the history angle, writing about the stone house on the Roberts farm, the first courthouse, the pioneer trails, the ferry house and river crossing. Lewis and Crystal Lake had enough history, Willey felt, to stack up well against whatever the competition.

His campaign continued throughout the summer of 1931. In July more details regarding the Conservation Commission's 25-year plan were disclosed. Proposed sites would soon be evaluated.

On August 6th the *Standard*, with Willey writing something to promote the state park idea nearly every week, carried the following article:

State Parks are in 3 classes: historical, recreational and scientific. Crystal Lake has two of the three in abundance. (Here Willey writes of the previously noted historical aspects of the Lewis and Crystal Lake area). He continues: *This writer came to Lewis 31 years ago. For many years prior to that folks came from 100 miles or more to vacation. Edgar Harlan is curator of the State Historical Department and we hope to see him in Lewis soon.*

Edgar Harlan agreed to come to Lewis. He was cordial. He did not make a commitment, and neither did he mention that he was being lobbied to distraction by politicians and big-money interests from historic and scenically breath-taking locations along the Mississippi river.

At Willey's urging, W.C. Boone, chairman of the Fish and Game Department, came through and took a look at Crystal Lake. Boone's impressions were not recorded, and were probably not that important. His area was game laws, not parks.

Regardless, Charles Willey felt these visits were a positive sign. They also came, for his paper, at an opportune time. Willey was becoming repetitive in his articles and now had something new.

Willey was out-and-about soliciting local support. The Cass County Farm Bureau signed on to his state park idea. Newspaper editors in Atlantic, Griswold, Anita and elsewhere wrote editorials favoring Willey's campaign.

Late that summer Willey renewed his plea regarding roads. No. 32, he wrote, was lost, and Lewis was forever poorer because of it, but a decision on No. 48 was still pending. Bringing it past the park and through Lewis would help offset the loss of No. 32. He would, as we now know, lose this argument as well. Willey seems to have given up, at that point, on roads.

Charley Willey loved baseball. He was a competitor. He'd lost every round of the road battle, and wanted to win something. The preservation of Crystal Lake became a crusade.

Willey spoke with Arden Mills of Atlantic, the area game warden. Mills is quoted as saying he not only favored a state part at Crystal Lake, he felt there should also be a fish hatchery. His idea was that the old "horseshoe" bayou, that channel of the East Nishnabotna remaining when the river was straightened, could be used. The bayou, Mills noted, was fed both by Deep Creek and the overflow from Crystal Lake. An outlet could be provided along with a few pumps and, for little cost, an ideal fish hatchery could be put into operation. Mills went on to tout the environmental benefits and noted that the hatchery he envisioned would create several jobs. With unemployment rates in 1931 standing at 16%, the potential of even a few jobs was inviting. (The idea of a fish hatchery is interesting, in part because many people believe Cold Springs lake is a hatchery. It is not, and never was. Instead, the DNR brings fingerlings to the lake, places them in cages to protect from predators, and feeds them until large enough to release.)

Willey thought so highly of Arden Mills, or at least his position on the park, that he began his lead story on September 16th by calling Mills "One of the greatest backers of a state park and hatchery..." A few days before this story appeared the Anita Tribune published an editorial giving the "greatest backer" status to Willey.

Arden Mills and Willey continued to converse. Mills probably had little, if any, influence with the Conservation Board, but he was local and people were fuzzy on the distinction between the board and the Department of Fish and Game. When Mills said it might help to circulate a petition in support of Crystal Lake becoming a state park, Willey acted.

He continued doing much more than writing newspaper articles. He toured the county that summer of '31, attending meetings, talked to local politicians and influential citizens. In late August Willey called for a meeting, originally to be held at the home of J. Frank Berry. The purpose was to organize a picnic and rally in support of a state park. During the rally, Willey suggested, thousands of signatures would be added to the petition. Interest was so great the planning meeting was moved to the school house. A committee was formed to detail plans and publicize the event, which would be held on a Sunday in late September. Willey and his committee invited Governor Dan Turner, representatives of the Board of Conservation, elected officials that included State Representative C. E. Malone of Atlantic. They arranged to have church services, a baseball double-header, a concert by the Tri-City band, and speeches from a few polished orators.

Willey had witnessed events at the lake that drew 10,000 people. He hoped to top that. He advertised, solicited, pleaded. His pitch was that this was the event that could convince the unconvinced. When the governor, members of the conservation board, high-ranking state politicians, saw how united southwest Iowans were in their support of the park they would surely be hard-pressed to say no.

Charles Willey was not a well man. He was then 66 years old. He was divorced. His only child, a daughter, lived in South Dakota. Willey's home was a back room in the office of his Standard. He was sick and he was going blind. His obituary refers to a long-term illness associated with the bladder. He also had cataracts; cataracts at a time when cataracts were much more difficult to deal with. Even then, in 1931, his eyesight had failed to the point that he was contemplating a surgical procedure that was radical and might well, he knew, leave him permanently sightless. These were perhaps factors that drove him to near-obsession. Crystal Lake would be the Woodward's legacy. His would be the preservation derived through achieving state park status.

Preparations for the Sunday rally were made by a group of Lewis volunteers. Limited by their work schedules and some rainy weather, Saturday evening arrived with much yet to be done. They toiled, some of them, until midnight. This was not a good omen. More bad news followed. The governor sent late word that he would not be able to attend. Game Warden Mills was there, but no one came from the State

Board of Conservation. Dignitaries who had agreed to speak cancelled out at the last minute. The show, though, would go on.

Office of the Lewis Standard.
The man bears a resemblance to Charles Willey, but is unidentified.

Lewis churches were dismissed after Sunday school and reconvened at the lake for a sermon delivered by the Congregational minister, Reverend Stark. Stark was followed by Charles Malone of Atlantic. State Representative Malone, a fine legislator but a man not known as a dynamic public speaker, had not originally been asked to deliver a keynote address. Lacking anyone else he was pressed into service. Newspaper accounts were generous. The *Telegraph* reported that Charles Malone "does not claim to be a public speaker, but when he is in a place like the one Sunday he is able to say a lot."

After Malone finished saying "a lot" the assemblage broke for picnic dinners. At 1 p.m. the band concert began. Afternoon arrivals increased. A large group came from Atlantic. In Griswold a long line of vehicles formed, most of them draped with signs proclaiming their love of Crystal Lake. One car had an old school bell mounted on the trunk and the bell clanged regularly as the cavalcade made the trip. Attendance was estimated at 7,000, probably an exaggerated figure and less than Willey had hoped for, but still a most impressive number.

Almost certainly the crowd would have been larger but for a black and threatening sky. The threat became reality just as the first baseball game was about to begin. When the storm hit, it did so with violence.

At the Will Bode farm west of the park shingles were torn from the roof and a hen house moved from its foundation. The Will Kunze place was pounded even harder; his windmill toppled and three chicken houses destroyed. Ray Butler lost the roof from his barn, and this is only a partial list of damaged property. At Crystal Lake branches came down as people scrambled for their cars or other shelter, and then the rain came. The deluge produced two inches in a short time.

Volunteers had agreed to circulate the petition Willey had prepared. Eventually they might have gotten the signature of everyone there, but the storm caught them well short. The petition, which Willey hoped would include 10,000 signatures or more, had only about 2,000. Others would sign, but the process was much delayed.

Chapter Eight

Whatever happens we will still have Crystal Lake.
It cannot be taken from us.

The rained-out baseball games were rescheduled for the following Sunday. Willey watched, although his failing eyesight made it difficult for him to follow the flight of the ball. The weather was pleasant, and as he sat in the bleachers there was opportunity to mull over an editorial he had been contemplating. His paper that week included an account of the games, the reprint of a *News Telegraph* piece about the benefits associated with Crystal Lake becoming a state park, and was followed by Willey's thoughts—words that reflect his weariness, the disappointment he felt over the failed picnic, his doubts, and the financial plight of his Lewis Standard.

"God himself provided Crystal Lake. It is a spot man naturally seeks for rest and relaxation. It cannot be removed. No man-made place can compare with His work. They are simply poor imitations and will always remain imitations.

We have just begun to fight. Whatever happens we will still have Crystal Lake. It cannot be taken from us.

We have and for some time have been passing through a Depression. Our advertising has declined to the point that we lose from $12-20 on every issue of the paper. We would like to stay in the game, but our weekly losses cannot be sustained.

If Charles Willey was feeling low as the winter of 1931-32 approached, depressed about the plight of his newspaper, his health, doubting if the state park would become a reality, he should have waited. Worse times were ahead. Willey had yet to encounter Jacob Crane.

As word of the 25-year plan spread more and more sportsmen, conservationists, campers, fishermen and picnickers, businessmen and the communities they lived in began to lobby for a state park. The Board of Conservation was under constant pressure; not just from lobbyists and voters, but from legislators wanting to take one home for their constituents.

The legislature moved to pass a state park appropriation. This was good news, although the money was for only an exploratory and feasibility study. Even so, being picked as a lucrative spot for a state park was an important step.

In part to put someone between them and the politics, in part because they recognized they lacked the expertise to evaluate topographical and watershed features that made some locations superior to others, the State Board of Conservation used much of the $25,000 appropriation to hire an expert to view suggested sites and compile a report that included recommendations.

A number of landscape engineers and architects made application. All those with acceptable credentials were given the opportunity to make a presentation. Each described how he would go about the survey, the report that would be provided, and answered questions.

Among the applicants was Jacob L. Crane, Jr. Crane was born in Michigan in 1892. After achieving a degree in landscape engineering at the University of Michigan he moved to Chicago. There, during the 1920s and into the 30s he engaged in private practice, mostly as a city planner.

Funds appropriated by the state legislature are generally not made available until July 1. This was the case with funding for the 25-year plan survey. In early July, 1931, Crane made his presentation. He made an impression and was awarded the contract.

Willey had probably never heard of Crane until that summer, but from July on the engineer from Chicago regularly made the pages of the *Lewis Standard*.

In November Willey and an informal committee consisting of J. Frank Berry and Mr. and Mrs. Fremont C. Jones went to Des Moines. The four people in that car were all about Lewis.

John Franklin Berry was born in Cass County in 1889 and came of age with the automobile. Berry knew the Model T, the Maxwells and early Buicks. He understood internal combustion engines and transmissions, could take things apart and fix them and put them back together. He would open a garage on the same building site as his home, buy a tow truck and go into business for himself. Berry was good at what he did—making a living and satisfying customers, repairing vehicles in the same location for 47 years. He was also an electrician, writing that he was one of the first in the area to practice this profession. It was away from the garage, however, that Berry was best known.

One snapshot of Frank Berry's life and times, one that illustrates the relationship Lewis residents had with the railroad, the river, flooding, and ties between men who had been, or would become, part of Crystal Lake, is given to us in an article published by the *Lewis Standard*. Years later the account was republished in the *Atlantic News Telegraph* and elaborated on by Ethyl Berry, Frank's wife and lifelong companion during his pursuit of local history.

The year was 1924. May had been wet, June even more so. The worst of it came in mid-month, when the Lewis newspaper reported that a Tuesday night downpour on already saturated soil put the winding, slow to drain Nishnabotna out of its banks, overflowing about 1,000 feet of Rock Island tracks. The floodwater rose and fell, subsiding gradually enough that tracks did not sustain major damage. But Thursday brought another heavy rain and previously drenched grade crumbled and shifted. Railroad crews labored to save the tracks but failed. A heavily loaded freight car overturned and the line shut down for several days.

That same Thursday afternoon Burleigh Painter, accompanied by his son-in-law Fred Schwingle and Fred's four-year-old son, Joe, set off for town to pick up the mail.

Burleigh and his son-in-law lived west of Lewis. The Nishnabotna was obviously out of its banks, but the bridge was high and dry. Burleigh was driving a strong team. The horses made it through swift but shallow water to the bridge and crossed, but on the east side muddy water over the unseen road was deeper. Horses were swept off the roadway, struggling to stay upright as they and the wagon were carried downstream. Within a few yards the team broke free and swam to shore, leaving Schwingle, Painter, and the boy floating in a swirling wagon box that was filling with water and threatening to capsize. As the wagon was carried southward it struck a telephone pole. Schwingle grabbed it and, as the wagon floated on, shinnied to the crossbar on top. Burleigh Painter watched for his chance and when the wagon box, now half full of water and threatening to tumble, struck a tree, he and the boy grabbed a branch.

A crowd quickly gathered on both banks, among them Bert Upson. He, with George Keffer and Charley Baker feeding him a rope, tried to reach the man on the pole. They came close, but the rising water kept them far enough from Schwingle that the line thrown fell short. Charles Baker and Frank Berry tried another approach, but could get no closer. Water continued to rise. Arvel Brown brought a rowboat and, assisted by Wilber Pierce and Ethan Allyn, spent about two hours of hard rowing, and several near misses, before finally reaching the tree and rescuing Burleigh Painter and the boy.

Schwingle, meanwhile, remained on top of the telephone pole. Darkness was approaching, more rain expected. While one boat was going for the man and boy in the tree, Frank Carr went to town and returned with his own rowboat. Carr, a Crystal Lake regular and former manager, was good with a boat and strong on the oars. Going with him was J. Frank Berry.

Maneuvering a rowboat in the whirling currents of a flooding river, dodging branches and uprooted trees, fighting surges easily capable of overturning a small craft, takes a bit of doing. At about 8 p.m., more than four hours after Schwingle grabbed the pole, Frank Berry got a rope on it. The overjoyed Schwingle jumped in the boat and Carr hauled for shore.

This incident not only brought together several men with close ties to the lake, men who would have a voice in shaping the future of the place. It was this flood, which nearly claimed three lives, that convinced county and state officials that the Nishnabotna had to be tamed. Blasting was soon to begin, the "Horseshoe" and the "Riffles" and other twists and turns and landmarks and fishing holes were eliminated. The geography of Crystal Lake and the surrounding area was permanently changed.

The riffles, at the top of the horseshoe, was usually ankle deep and easily waded by those taking the scenic route to Crystal Lake. Water downstream was deeper, a fine location for boating and courting. The horseshoe was eliminated when the river was straightened.

Berry's obituary tells us he served as secretary of the Lewis Cemetery Association for 42 years. He was a long-time member of the volunteer fire department, including 22 years as chief. He was a historian and photographer who learned as much in the field as he did in museums and libraries and the courthouse. Berry was scoutmaster of Lewis Troop 66 from the late 1930s into the 1950s. Boys in Berry's charge learned ropes and camping and outdoor lore. They tied the sheepshank and bowline and square knot and memorized the scout oath and motto. Berry insisted his scouts "do their duty, to God and to country."

One great attraction of scouting under J. Frank Berry was field trips. He took his boys to the old grist mill on Indian creek, pointed out where the dam and paddle-wheel had been. He showed them the Mormon trail, Indian burial grounds, the council house and village sites. During his lifetime he found hundreds of arrowheads and other Indian artifacts and he was glad to show his scouts the best places to look.

Berry's life-long pursuit of local history got its start, or at least a healthy boost, in 1920. Then thirty-one years of age and a family man, he bought the former Lewis cheese plant. Berry tore down the structure and used the lumber to build the house he and Ethyl called home for the rest of their lives.

While his work as an electrician was sporadic, it offered opportunities for his historic interest. He recounted installing wiring, in the 1920s and 30s, in houses built half a century earlier. His work required him to spend time in the attics of these homes, where he found treasurers galore. Some he purchased, others were given away by owners glad to have their attics cleaned out.

Frank Berry studied history of all types. He was deeply interested in Ann Rutledge and her relationship with Abraham Lincoln. He acquired a lock of her hair, a relic he enjoyed displaying to guests. His focus, though, was Cass County, particularly the Lewis area. Berry walked and diagrammed the streets of Indiantown and Iranistan, determined who lived where and when, where they died and how.

For decades Berry spent his leisure time tracing the old trails, wandering farm fields after crops were out in the fall and following heavy rains in the spring, looking for relics and indentations and ruts and evidence of crossings. The original Mormon trail, the main route, had been mapped earlier. The "handcart trail," a secondary road for a special purpose, was not so easy. Berry's quest of Mormon trails led him all the way to Salt Lake City, where he studied the construction of a handcart. He would return to Lewis and, with help from Ed Kunze, build a replica that was displayed for a time in the downtown park.

He thirsted for ever more information, particularly on Native Americans. His writing tends to dismiss tribes relocated here by treaty as "reservation Indians." While he sympathized with their plight, he was drawn more by the tribes that had inhabited this area hundreds and even many thousands of years before. In a column written for the *Telegraph* in 1969 he reveals his frustration at this lack of knowledge.

Written history available to Berry held that Indians (if you prefer the term "Native Americans" feel free to substitute) had inhabited this area for at least 10,000 to 12,000 years, yet made little impact. Indians, according to high school history, tread softly, changed little, and left scarcely a footprint.

In 1897, when Berry was in third grade, the Werner School Book Company published a history of Iowa that was widely used in our public school system. Indians are scarcely mentioned. Lafe Young's 1877 History of Cass County refers to the area's first inhabitants as being Indians, then briefly and superficially delves into tribes that were moved here, and later moved away, as a result of land treaties.

These accounts are typical. The *Iowa Official Register* contains a history of our state written by Dorothy Schwieder, then a professor of history at Iowa State University. Ms. Schwieder, a noted Iowa historian and author of several books writes, as have others, that in 1673 Marquette and Joliet were the first whites to set foot in what is now Iowa. Prior to 1673, she tells us, Iowa was occupied by "approximately 17 different Indian tribes."

The statement strikes me as absurd. Understanding, as Ms. Schwieder surely did, that Indians inhabited this area for more than 10,000 years—some are now saying twice that long—knowing that feuds and war and cyclical changes in climate, their own nomadic tendencies, caused Indians to relocate; that cultures rise and fall to be replaced by another, and yet to presume to know how many tribes had lived here is an incredibly dismissive view.

Charles C. Mann, in his book *1491* (Vintage Books, published 2005) writes that the inadequacy of these histories has various explanations: Authors are anxious to get to the purpose, which is generally the period beginning with white settlement. Dealing with the "Indian Problem" was distasteful, but necessary, and is difficult to dwell on without reflecting negatively upon noted historic (white) figures. Mann also points out that knowledge was, and remains, limited. Indians who inhabited the plains thousands of years ago did not build pyramids, nor did they have a written language.

Today, while we know more than during Berry's time, much remains unknown. Monte Verde, a riverbank in Chile, was excavated in the 1970s and 80s. Reports of this dig state findings of "suggestive indications" of human habitation more than 32,000 years ago. This, coupled with the generally accepted theory that these people arrived in North American by walking across the Bering Strait and, generation after generation, migrated ever farther southward, suggests they were here before they arrived in Chili. We know Indian cultures on the east coast built major cities, managed extensive farms, had a system of government that had been refined over centuries. We know that plains Indians practiced game management, that some tribes raised crops to an extent not previously expected and were therefore only somewhat nomadic. They improved grassland by routinely burning the prairies. We also know that Europeans, before and after Columbus, brought smallpox and other diseases for which Indians had no resistance. In the period between Columbus and white settlement thousands, probably millions, of Indians perished in one plague or another. Entire tribes were wiped out, cities abandoned. What Lewis and Clark found was only a remnant of what had been.

Berry understood that the hills he walked had been trod by others—that white history was but a speck of sand.

In the mid 1950s he pointed out to his Boy Scout troop a place that once was. On Deep Creek, near the springs and sandstone bluff, had been an Indian village. He knew this because of the quantity of stone tools he'd found there. He showed some of them to us. Many were delicately made, some more crude; an indication, Berry suspected, that more than one culture lived there, occupying the place perhaps hundreds or even thousands of years apart. In either case, he wanted us to appreciate that these tools were not those of later tribes; tribes spoiled by white trade goods. He was frustrated that he did not more about them, writing that when asked of the Indians who lived here he could not give more than a partial answer. It was the relics of these tribes, clues to who they were and how they lived, that he searched for. He recognized that Crystal Lake, important in his time as an amusement park and picnic area, attracted people long before the Vikings or Columbus or the French set foot on what was called the Americas. When Berry went to the bluff above the springs, viewed the sandstone ledges and the expanse of timber and wetland to the Nishnabotna, he heard echoes of the past—the very distant past.

F.C. "Mont" Jones was, at the time of his trip to Des Moines with Willey and Berry, 75 years old. Born in New York in 1856, he came to Iowa at the age of 17. He later married Georgia Teft, of the Teft family that operated the ferry west of Lewis. Jones farmed north of town, retiring in 1909. He and Georgia moved to Lewis and became active in community affairs. Jones became noted for his intricate woodwork, often pieces of furniture in miniature. He and Georgia were a few years younger than Belle and Chet Woodward, but were well acquainted. One of their sons, Dr. C.R. Jones, founded and managed the Jones Hospital in Atlantic. The Jones family had been regulars at Crystal Lake since the time it was built. When Willey looked for support, and a driver, Berry and the Joneses were more than willing,

They took with them the petition supporting the acquisition of Crystal Lake for a state park. It carried 3,500 signatures. Willey had hoped for more, a lot more, but when the rally was rained out and signers had to be solicited one by one the process was a slow one. Willey, knowing site evaluations were already underway, did not feel it wise to wait any longer.

Nothing much was decided by the meeting. The Board of Conservation accepted the petition, let the delegation from Lewis know that Jacob Crane was doing the survey, that his expert recommendations would carry considerable weight.

Would Crane come to Lewis? Would he at least look at Crystal Lake? Willey, J. Frank Berry, and Mont and Georgia Jones left feeling they had a promise that the board would assure that Crane would include Lewis on his agenda.

Willey kept up the pressure, making regular phone calls to the commission office. He was also sending them copies of his articles and those of county newspapers that advocated the state park. He obtained Crane's Chicago address and sent him copies as well.

There were a lot of articles to send. Willey kept doing them, week after week, even when there was nothing new to report. In early December he wrote that "Governor Dan Turner wants to make it possible for every citizen to use fully Iowa's natural resources." This was hardly news. Daniel Webster Turner, born near Corning, was a one-term governor who campaigned as an advocate of conservation, spoke often of increasing the number of state parks.

The following week Willey wrote of Jacob Crane, what his survey was, the promise that he'd view Crystal Lake. Willey concluded by saying he "was still waiting."

Willey wrote again the following week, depicting once more the natural beauty of the sandstone bluff, the sparkling and abundant supply of pure spring water, the historical locations in the immediate vicinity. This was probably for Crane's benefit, as subscribers could hardly have avoided Willey's previous articles touting the same benefits. The following week

Willey penned yet another article that again went into depth on local history, the Underground Railroad, the first county seat. All of these articles were mailed to both Crane and o members of the conservation board.

Willey finally received the phone call he'd been waiting for: Crane is on the way and will be in Lewis that day. Willey is prepared. He, J. Frank Berry, along with F.C. and Mrs. Jones, have an agenda. They want Crane to see the entire park, not just the one-acre lake. They plan to give him a tour of the area, pointing out pioneer trails, the stone house, the east end park in Lewis, the original courthouse and the old stage stop. There was some concern about actually getting to Crystal Lake. The weather had been bad—rain mixed with snow for two or three days. The road south of town, not yet graveled, was a bog. Frank Berry had a garage and tow truck, so presumably he had a way. Crane, however, did not show up. Willey and his group saw morning turn to afternoon and afternoon to evening with no landscape engineer.

Willey is careful in what he writes about the incident. If he wasn't furious he was deeply disappointed. He telephoned the Board of Conservation. All they could tell him is that Crane had Crystal Lake on his agenda for that day. Someone would talk to him. Crane responded by letter. He had, he said, been to Crystal Lake. But because the roads were so bad he did not have time to stop at the newspaper office, did not perceive the need to see anyone in order to evaluate the site. That evaluation, Crane stated, was not good. The place was not suitable for a state park. His exact words, as quoted in the paper, were that he "was not in a position to recommend Crystal Lake."

Willey reported the rejection, writing that Crane lacked information, he did not take the tour of historic sites, and further that given the condition of roads no one could have made an in-depth assessment. Willey does not say outright what a few suspected—the Crane didn't even come to Lewis—but the implication is there. The state, Willey must have thought, had belittled his town once again.

A couple of noteworthy things came out of this little difficulty. Crane, a Chicago Democrat, apparently got a lesson in Iowa Republican politics. He would also write something that caused park advocates to chart a course they had not previously considered.

In Crane's letter he wrote that funding of parks was an issue to be "worked out." One of the sites under consideration was near Ottumwa, and residents of that area had offered financial aid to the board. Crane concluded that, for monetary reasons, the Ottumwa project would be recommended.

Crane was soon to have a change of heart with regard to Crystal Lake. He had been, we must assume, the recipient of some advice. Willey's unfavorable articles, the brush-off Crane had given the Lewis group, had attracted the attention of a number of influential Atlantic residents. One of them was Harry Swan. Swan, a prominent attorney and president of the local Isaac Walton chapter, was active in Republican politics. Swan would become a worker in the Crystal Lake/state park effort, serve on a committee to raise funds and convince the Conservation Board. He was on a first-name basis with leading Iowa Republicans, including Governor Dan Turner. The fact that state-appropriated dollars for a survey that didn't seem that difficult were going to an out-of-state Democrat may have been annoying. When that Democrat slighted a good Republican newspaper editor, dismissed the beloved Crystal Lake as unsuitable, then that person might need some direction. Precisely what took place we do not know. We do know, however, that by late February Mr. Crane was letting it be circulated that he'd modified his stance. Warden Mills told Willey he had it on good authority that Jacob Crane had changed his mind and would, after all, look favorably on Crystal Lake.

There may also have been a suggestion that Crane write to Willey and patch things up a bit. Whether told to or not, Crane wrote Willey a letter. While somewhat sarcastic and perhaps a bit condescending, the letter offered hope that earlier public statements by Crane had not.

Dear Sir,

It has been kind of you to send me copies of the Standard containing comments on the state park situation in that section of Iowa and I trust that the people of that community understand that we are making a special survey of the southwest-central territory to determine the best possibilities for a state park.

Meanwhile we can not commit ourselves for or against any one site, such as Crystal Lake, and we have not yet made any recommendation with reference to that particular property. I must say that on the visit to Crystal Lake I was impressed by the unusual features and we shall probably recommend that it be made permanently available to the public in some manner even if it does not become a state park.

I shall be glad to have you publish this letter and I hope you will see that the material in the Standard with reference to Crystal Lake be reasonable and of such nature to keep the attitude of your readers unprejudiced until the matter can be resolved in a sensible way.

(SIGNED) *Jacob L. Crane, Jr.*

Crane went about his survey in other parts of the state. In Lewis the group of Willey, Berry, Jones, Bill Zyke and others weighed the fact that, despite noble pronouncements by the Board of Conservation, Crane's letter implied that the best chance for a state park was to pay the price. Ottumwa was putting up money. Ottumwa, Crane said, would get a park.

Willey was tired and he was sick. He wrote that nothing would be resolved in the near future. Crane promised that Crystal Lake would be recommended for something, but what that something was wouldn't be known until his report was made public, which wouldn't be until the legislature had seen it. The General Assembly would not reconvene until January of 1933. Willey was not sure where he'd be by that time.

Willey's health continued to fail, and at the same time economic woes of the Great Depression made it ever-more difficult to operate his newspaper. As businesses went under the life-blood of the paper, paid advertisements, diminished. When Willey wrote in 1931 that he was losing money on every edition there is no reason to doubt him. Yet when the *Lewis Standard* ceased to be it was not, according to Willey, because he'd gone broke.

In the final edition he wrote that his 32 years with the paper, which included 13 as publisher and proprietor, were ending due to health. He was, he continued, having surgery on his left eye and, shortly thereafter, the right. "I may see you again," he concluded, "but maybe not."

The paper sold to F.W. Hanton, publisher, editor and owner of the *Griswold American*.

Chapter Nine

*The town marshal, a dog in hot pursuit, took refuge
on John Jayberg's front porch*

Jacob Crane's report was delivered to the legislature, then became available to the public in the summer of 1933. In August bound volumes of all 176 pages were presented to libraries across the state, there to gather dust. The book is a tedious read, which may help explain why local newspapers—so interested in summer of 1931—gave it little attention. Crane starts his book with a discourse on the purpose and importance of the survey. He speaks glowingly, as he does throughout, of the two state agencies having a responsibility for conservation; the State Board of Conservation and the Fish and Game Commission. He does not say so, but we draw the implication that the wisdom of these agencies was demonstrated in the hiring of Crane. The man had no small opinion of himself, nor the role of government. He writes that public recreation must be provided for by the government, ranking it with public health, public safety, public highways. He uses Europe as a model, taking the position that government control of land will come here just as it had there. He writes that Iowa was in a state of transition, moving from "a pioneer to civilized state of affairs." A full chapter is devoted to the origin, range and limitations of the plan, another on how it was conducted, followed by chapters on Iowa demographics and history.

He has general plans for the conservation of soil, water, and wildlife, tells us the compilation of the plan required 40,000 miles of travel about the state, visitation of 2,000 sites, all of which were closely evaluated. A section is devoted to definitions, which tend to be somewhat blurred. He believes state parks are one thing, state refuges another, and also offered plans for scenic preserves and roadside parks and public hunting areas.

He works out formulas based on projected population trends to provide recommendations on what should go where. He plans for 38 lakes, seven proposed state parks, dozens of historic preserves, scientific preserves, scenic areas, forest preserves, power pond preserves and sanctuaries for both plants and wildlife. Crane stressed that state parks should be large—preferably 1.000 acres or more. Parks were to offer multiple recreational opportunities and should be prepared, he believed, to handle tens of thousands of people. He recommended that parks be spaced approximately 80 miles apart so attendees would not have to drive more than forty miles. He makes numerous references to the limited funding available to the Board of Conservation, and cites the same consideration he stressed to Charles Willey: communities willing to help with financing would be deserving of special consideration.

Crane does not, anywhere in the book, make specific reference to Crystal Lake. What he does show is a symbol on several maps designating western Cass County as being the site of a "planned major artificial lake." Given the fact that Crane writes in detail about other sites, other lakes, other preserves, even to the extent of providing cost estimates, his lack of any other reference make it appear doubtful he seriously contemplated Crystal Lake as the site of anything. Also worth noting is that the symbol on his maps has the "major artificial lake" in Cass County a mile or more west of the Nishnabotna. Crystal Lake was always east of the river; after the Nishnabotna was straightened it became even farther east.

Charles Willey could not read the report. The cataract surgery had not been a success. Hanton later wrote an article saying the ordeal had broken Willey's health. This may have been, yet through the summer of '33 he was a regular at Crystal Lake baseball games. Cab Marker had another solid team, and if Willey couldn't see he could hear. Stories were told of the pleasure he derived from the sound of a solid hit, infield chatter, the pop of a Porter fast ball slapping into a beefsteak-stuffed mitt.

Another article in the Lewis news section of Hanton's *Griswold American* refers to a narrow escape. Someone reported a vicious dog on the loose in Lewis's downtown park, a dog that allegedly bit—or tried to bite—a boy on a bicycle. Town marshal Marxen responded. Upon arrival the dog, which actually was vicious, turned on Marxen. The town marshal, a dog in hot pursuit, took refuge on the porch of the John Jayberg home. The dog returned to the park. While this was going on Charles Willey, blind, was on a bench where he had gone to enjoy the afternoon sun. He could hear barking, shouts and general excitement going on around him. Not knowing where to go, or where the dog was, he remained seated. The dog either didn't notice or wasn't interested in a stationary victim.

While Crane's report was summarized in a few newspapers, particularly those in areas that were given specifics on a recommended project in their community, the wait had been long and attention turned elsewhere. The Great Depression was deepening. The state was low on money. Crane's plan of paying for what he called a 5.5 million dollar project (that estimate was absurdly low) called for more taxes and a good deal of general fund money. With the revenue to the state's general fund as dry as the old river channel, not much of Crane's plan seemed likely to happen anytime soon.

Jacob Crane went on to other things. In 1937 he became a part of the rapidly growing federal government. He served as an assistant administrator in a bureaucracy created to provide housing for defense workers. A strong advocate of government subsidized housing, he was later appointed to a high level position in the U.S. Housing Authority. He spent the remainder of his career with the federal government, and died in 1988 at the age of 97.

In 1919 original members of Board of Conservation liked the Loess Hills and Lake Manawa, but found not much else in southwest Iowa that offered promise in the way of a state park. Jacob Crane, twelve years later, concurred. Appropriation requests submitted by the Board of Conservation had not, and never would, include funding to purchase Crystal Lake.

Chapter Ten - 1934

They would, however, designate it as a state park if the land was donated

When Charles Willey was forced to give up his *Standard* the effort for a state park lost, for a time, momentum. We suspect a healthy Willey would have pounced on Crane's report, railed about what it didn't say regarding Crystal Lake, make another call on the Board of Conservation, have a few words with state legislators, but he was in no condition to do any of that. In April of 1934, less than two years after his forced retirement, Willey died. He had been a patient at Jones Hospital in Atlantic; suffering, blind, with loyal friends who visited but most often alone, always in pain, for several weeks. Obituaries spoke of his good deeds, of a man who was never approached by someone down-and-out without giving them the price of a meal. He had been a true patriot during World War I. He was active with the Red Cross. Karl McDonald, proprietor of McDonald's Hamburger Shop in Lewis, remembered Willey as a true friend. His death was a reminder of a project Willey had put in motion, a project that was still without resolution.

Picnic season was approaching. Bert Upson would soon be opening Crystal Lake. Chet Woodward was getting older. It was time to get on with the work Willey had started.

In June, with grass beginning to grow on Willey's grave, a group of men from every part of Cass County met in Atlantic. Willey had promoted the state park from the standpoint of historic preservation and recreation. Others saw it as a conservation issue. The men who met in mid-June of 1934 concurred, and they had another angle—jobs.

The Cass County Emergency Relief Committee oversaw a variety of projects that included subsistence gardens, a program wherein they identified and prepared vacant lots for gardening, then distributed free seeds to the needy and assigned them garden space. The Committee played a role in administrating local, state and federal welfare programs, and they did what they could to help men find work.

When F.W. Hanton bought the *Standard* he bought the subscription list and made every effort to retain the good will of those who had advertised in Willey's newspaper. He featured, front page, right column, *Lewis News*, with few exceptions doing so in every edition for several years. He also had a Lewis section on page two for social events and school news. Between the time he bought the *Standard* in 1931 and the summer of 1934, Hanton had next to nothing to say about Crystal Lake. But beginning with his coverage of the June meeting in Atlantic he takes up where Willey left off.

His lead story on June 20, 1934:

For years it has been the dream of many to have Crystal Lake pass into the hands of the state Conservation and a state park established in Cass County. Much work and effort has been put forth and at times it looked like the goal was near, only to be disappointed.

The last movement has been under way for several days and Friday night a large number of men gathered at Atlantic and perfected a temporary organization to get the matter under way. . . . The project is being sponsored by the Cass County Emergency relief committee and if it is put across there will be work for the unemployed and in this manner the poor will be able to at least get enough money to keep their families during the coming fall and winter. Cass County has perhaps 150 men who have depended on work of some kind to furnish food for their families. By securing this tract of land the men would be given employment a part of the time.

Hanton goes on to explain that he has spoken with state officials and been told there was no interest in buying the sixty acre tract. The state would, however, designate it a state park if the land was donated. Chet Woodward was in favor. He placed a value on the land, lake, skating rink, baseball diamond and other facilities at a reasonable $6,000. He opened donations with $1,000, reducing the amount to be raised to $5,000.

Burdette Roland of Atlantic was named president of the temporary organization. Arden Mills, the game warden, was Secretary. Other officers and committee members included Robert Graham, John Cruise, William Zike of Lewis, Walter Budd and Noel Seney from Massena, F.W. Hanton of Griswold, Bert Stone from Cumberland, C.E. Robinson of Wiota, L.W. Wheatley of Marne, A.N. Sein of Lorah, Eno Shroder of Lyman and Robert Bell from Fletcher Chapel.

The group felt a sense of urgency. Chet Woodward gave them a deadline; his price, and offer of $1,000, was good only until March 1, less than a year away.

The "temporary" committee formed in June obtained pledges for only a small amount of money, and perhaps getting the ball rolling was all they hoped for. Raising five thousand dollars during Depression years was not easy. By late summer the impetus again stalled; fund-raising had all but ceased.

In November leadership was turned over to some of the heaviest hitters in the county. Another meeting was held, this one in the Cameo Room of the Hotel Whitney on a Friday night shortly before Thanksgiving. Presiding was Harry Bryant Swan.

Swan was born in Atlantic in 1894, studied law and was admitted to the bar at the age of 21. A year later he enlisted for the war in France, then came home to resume his law practice. He was the first commander of the 9th District American Legion. Swan was a member of the Masonic Lodge and Scottish Rite. Active in politics from his youth, Swan would become state chairman of the Iowa Republican party, receive consideration for national chair. He ran unsuccessfully for the office of Iowa Attorney General. He took in Boyd Cambridge as his law partner. He was president of the local chapter of Isaac Walton. When Swan was killed in a car accident in 1941 Governor Bourke B. Hickenlooper came to Atlantic to deliver the keynote address. Atlantic's Congregational church could not begin to hold the crowd for his funeral. At least a couple of hundred stood outside the church, while several hundred others were in or on the lawn of the Roland, Baxter & Peacock funeral home, which had been wired with speakers indoors and out for this occasion. Honorary pallbearers included a former governor and a U.S. Congressman.

In 1934 Harry Swan was in his prime and, from a political standpoint, in a position to make things happen. Harry Swan knew, as pundits said, where the bear hid in the woods. He knew all about Crane and the 25-year plan and he understood very well the workings of the Conservation Board. He had been involved behind the scenes for some time, had apparently obtained a commitment. At the Hotel Whitney meeting he explained that he had conversed with "people in a position to know" and that the reluctance to convert Crystal Lake to a state park went beyond money. Already established was the fact that the Board would not consider Crystal Lake unless it was given to them, and even if such was to happen there was reluctance to make it a state park. Jacob Crane's report, which the Board had accepted and was acting on, called for state parks to consist of several hundred acres, preferably 1,000 or more. Sixty acres was not enough. However, Swan said, and this was critically important, if funds were raised to buy the park he had every reason to believe it would be accepted and the state would then move to acquire additional land. Swan suggested a close accounting of all donations and, should the state "fail to exercise their option," the money would be returned.

This sounded reasonable but there was a problem—the state had not one option to exercise, but two. Fulfilling the first was simply to accept 60 acres, a lake and amusement park, as a gift. This cost the state nothing. Once they'd accepted the money was spent and there'd be no refunds. The state could call the place anything they wanted—even a state park if that made people in Cass County happy. The board, however, was purely on their honor to follow through on what Harry Swan took as a promise to treat the place as a first-rate facility and acquire several hundred acres of additional land.

It seems likely that a lawyer, and Swan was a good one, would have the agreement reduced to writing, just as was done when the state accepted Wildcat Den and other park land. For whatever reason, this was not done.

While Swan presided over the meeting, pledged his support and offered his services as an attorney, he preferred not to be an officer of the committee.

Elected chair was Howard A. Marshall of Atlantic. Marshall's resume was as impressive as Swan's. Marshall graduated from Atlantic high school in 1906, attended first the University of Michigan, later Grinnell College in Iowa. An outstanding high school athlete, he was a three-year starting quarterback at Grinnell. He was just as good in track, basketball and baseball—good enough to be offered a contract to play professionally. He labored in baseball's minor leagues for five years, then returned to Atlantic, taking a job at the Herring Motor company. Clyde Herring, owner of the business, was a staunch Democrat, as involved in politics as was Harry Swan.

In 1920 Marshall left Herring's Ford dealership to assist W.E. Kelloway in organizing the Walnut Grove Corporation, of which he was named manager. In 1925 he moved up to vice-president and, in 1936, president. He served as a director of the Whitney Loan & Trust company, was at one time chairman of the Atlantic Memorial Hospital fund, active in Rotary, the Masonic lodge, and Elks.

Harry Swan had Republican connections galore. Howard Marshall knew the Democrat, Clyde Herring, who made Dan Turner a one-term governor.

The committee was comprised of at least one member from each town in the county, and all were respected leaders. Harry Jordan of Wiota was a former county sheriff. Three (E.C. Montgomery of Atlantic, F.N. Hobson of Griswold, and D.J. Chalmers of Grant) were doctors. Grant, of course, is not in Cass County, but when plans became known several citizens of that town, having enjoyed Crystal Lake for years, asked to participate.

Leslie Hodges operated Hodges Furniture and Funeral Home in Cumberland for over 50 years. A.A. Gillette was selected, Glen Roe from Anita, Eno Schroeder from Lyman and, because he was an influential and well-known cattle baron and could be counted on for a sizeable donation, Wayland A. Hopley was added. G.T. "Gus" Kuester from Griswold had been elected to the state legislature earlier that month. He would not become a State Representative until January but he would, he promised, go to Des Moines committed in support of a state park for Cass County.

The representative from Lewis was Clarence W. Hancock. Hancock was born on a farm near Crystal Lake in 1907. He graduated from Lewis High School, worked for several years at the Citizen's State Bank in Lewis, then went into business for himself by opening a main street insurance office. He was commander of a tank unit during World War ll, served as the city treasurer, was a long-time member and president of the school board, held several church offices and supported the Lewis community in a way only a few other people have.

Hancock married Veryl Smiley. She served as his office assistant for decades. Those who knew the Hancocks superficially, as their insurance agent or tax accountant, found them quiet, competent, as refined as British royalty. Randall Breckerbaumer, who became a partner in Hancock's agency in 1963 and worked with them for nearly thirty years, says they were all that and more.

"In all those years of working together," Breckerbaumer said, "We never had a harsh word. Not even one."

His wife, Sharon Casady Breckerbaumer, remembers a Clarence Hancock who would not quarrel or speak badly of anyone. He'd done all the fighting he cared to during the war.

"He used to say," Randall laughs, "that there was nothing to be gained by 'pissing in front of a skunk.' He believed it, and he lived it."

There was more to Hancock than impeccable manners. He could tell a story, when the time and audience was right, with a deftness of word and expression that was all his own. The story might soon be forgotten—the delivery was not.

Hancock was a health food eccentric. In his office was a refrigerator crammed with alfalfa sprouts, flax and bran and quinoa. Shelves were lined with bottles and bags. He consumed quantities of vitamins, minerals, supplements, and encouraged Randall to do likewise. Breckerbaumer describes trying a paste that tasted awful, of wondering how Clarence Hancock could possibly eat the stuff. But he became a convert and still buys from the same supplier Hancock used. (For the record, Randall Breckerbaumer looks much younger than he is.)

Members of that 1934 group, which called themselves and their mission "The Crystal Lake Project," would come and go. Some worked harder than others, some gave up, saw the mission as being completed when it was not. Clarence Hancock was among those who stayed the course.

In November of 1934, with the "Crystal Lake Project" underway, Chet Woodward celebrated his 89th birthday.

Pavilion as originally built by Belle and Chet Woodward.

Pavilion after being rebuilt in the late 1930s.

Chapter Eleven – 1935

The Lewis semi-pro Maidens thumped Marne, 21-7

Not much in the way of fundraising was done during the holiday season but by mid-January, with temperatures dropping below zero night after night, the lake project heated up. Each member of the committee was to form a sub-committee in their respective towns and solicit by personal contact, arrange for benefit dinners and other events. Chet's deadline, all were reminded, was March 1.

The superintendent of the Lewis School was a popular young educator and family man named Jake Riekena. Jake didn't need encouragement from his board president (Clarence Hancock) to proclaim that support would be from both himself and the school. Classes from the Lewis school had held countless picnics at Crystal Lake over the previous 37 years, as had teachers and the school board. It was only right, Reikena told the *Griswold American*, that the school do what could be done. He made plans for an evening of basketball in the school gymnasium. Several games would be played, abbreviated contests that promised to attract more than just students and the families of participants. One game would pit the Lewis girls, a pretty good team, against their fathers. The event was scheduled for January 30.

A few nights prior to that the executive committee of the "Crystal Lake Project" met again at the Hotel Whitney. Harry Swan again presided. Pledges and actual donations had reached $1,000. Swan and Marshall believed, or at least said they believed, that raising one-fifth of the amount needed in such a short time was a promising indication of success.

The evening of January 30 was cold and snowy and attendance at the basketball benefit was not what it might have been. The main event—the girls taking on their fathers in a six-on-six contest played by girl's rules, presented a problem. Not all of the girls on the team had a father that was up to the challenge. Only five agreed to play. Supt. Riekena, always a good sport, said he'd fill in.

The girls, clearly better at the game and considerably younger, took the lead. Reikena, trying to keep the score from becoming an embarrassment, made a move for the basket that was perhaps not advisable. He slipped, fell, and broke his collarbone. The game ended early. A newspaper article said Mrs. Reikena was the big loser—she not only had two young children to care for, she had a husband who couldn't tie his own shoelaces.

Riedkena's basketball idea caught on. On February 12th Griswold hosted Massena for both a boys and girls high school benefit game. A group called "The Hillbilly Band" from Lyman offered to entertain before the game and again at half-time. They featured "Tiny" Kistler, "The All-American Girl," and it was promised that she'd dazzle the crowd with her creative dance numbers. A few more dollars were handed over to the committee.

Later that month Cab Marker, better known for his baseball teams, put together two basketball squads, one comprised of men, the other not. He issued a challenge to Marne to do the same, offering to play them on the Marne court. The women from Lewis, calling themselves the "Lewis Semi-Pro Maidens," thumped Marne 21-7. The Lewis men had a closer game, prevailing by 26-20. All profit, of which there was not a great deal, went to the lake project.

Church dinners raised a few more dollars, but the March 1st deadline came and went and less than half the $5,000 had been raised. Again, the effort lagged. Chet Woodward was willing to grant an extension—the problem was that in 1935 money was scarce. People gave and gave again. While a few contributed a substantial amount, most donations came in nickels and dimes. It takes a lot of pocket change to make $5,000.

Crystal Lake opened on schedule, Burt Upson again the manager. Picnickers and campers were there in numbers. The Misses Caroline and Margaret Weaver came from Exeter Nebr., to meet with relatives from the Kennedy and Burnside family. They may have noticed that facilities were showing signs of slipping. The roof on the pavilion was sagging, the floor in the roller-skating rink was not in the best shape. Rental skates and rental bathing uniforms were wearing out. Upson did what he could, but his role was manager. He did not make capital improvements. This was Chet Woodward's place. Chet was approaching 90, his interest had ebbed when Belle died. He did not spend money unnecessarily. He'd set a price, the committee—providing funds could be raised—had accepted. There was little incentive for him to invest in improvements.

A near-tragedy struck in mid-July. Two teen-age girls, unnamed in newspaper articles, leaped into the deep end of the lake. They could not swim, didn't realize they were in over their heads, and panicked. They went under, righted themselves and bobbed to the surface, floundered, screamed for help, then went under again. Two local boys, Forest Sperry and Morris Wilson, were quick to the rescue.

Burt Upson had been lifeguard for years. If he was ever called upon to save someone we find no record of it. Then, while he was dealing with dirty bathing suits and a shortage of picnic tables, two kids made the front page with an account that gives them hero status.

In mid-August the "Crystal Lake Project" committee, accompanied by dozens of farmers and businessmen, converged on the courthouse to meet with the County Board of Supervisors. Their plea was for money. It was pointed out that Carroll County supervisors had voted to expend funds for a similar project, therefore it seemed reasonable that Cass County do so as well. The supervisors agreed to help, and would do so (they later contributed $2,000), but insisted the committee first go back to the public. They did. More church dinners were scheduled. Another door-to-door canvas took place. Cab Marker, who had already had benefit baseball games, had another. Both the Atlantic and Griswold newspapers printed front-page articles touting the benefits of Crystal Lake as a state park, urging readers to contribute, and for those who had already done so to do it again.

In early September the Atlantic City Council wrote a check for the final $800 needed to reach the goal. Headlines were joyous. Those who had worked, contributed, planned, and worked some more were elated. Women of the three Lewis churches, who had combined to plan a chicken and biscuit fund-raiser for later that month, called the event off.

It would take a few days for Harry Swan and the assistant AG representing the state to complete legal necessities of a clear title, abstract and deed. These matters were expedited and on September 25 the *Telegraph's* front page, left column lead announced that Crystal Lake was—at long last—a state park. Charles Willey would have been jubilant.

The fly in the ointment, which it seems neither the newspaper editors nor anyone else was considering at the time, was that all the state had done was accept a generous gift. The assumption was that they'd soon make good on the promise Harry Swan said he'd extracted. They did not.

Chapter Twelve - 1936-37

*Rowdiness would not be tolerated anytime
of the day or night*

Newspaper accounts published in the fall of 1935 quoted a source with the Board of Conservation as saying improvements would be underway soon; probably before winter.

Winter came and went without any indication of a state presence. No mowing, maintenance or work of any kind was undertaken. There was no caretaker. Some vandalism took place. Spring came and with it the approach of what had, for forty years, been a busy time for Crystal Lake, yet there was no one home. All the state had done that anyone could discern was change the name.

In mid-May a delegation, including "Mont" and Georgia Jones and J. Frank Berry, made another trip to Des Moines, this time to visit with Governor Herring. They voiced a complaint that would be made time and time again during the years to come—that promises made were not being kept.

One item that emerges from a news article on the meeting is that Herring was told it was the understanding of a committee that included Harry Swan that, in addition to funding for maintenance, "a sum of money had been set aside by the state for the purchase of additional land." The land in question laid to the west, between the park and the river, and it was available at a realistic price. The message was delivered: area residents had fulfilled their part, now the state needed to do theirs.

The commission had to do some serious work to prepare Cold Springs for the summer season, and they needed to move to buy the land they'd agreed to buy.

Governor Herring said he'd look into it. We presume he did. We further presume commissioners told the governor they had no people or money for the job.

We can only speculate on exactly who promised what, and if money had been set aside, where did it go? Why wasn't there a written agreement detailing the state's obligations, which had been standard in other transfers of this type?

Regardless, within a couple of days of the meeting the Lewis city council heard from the commission. An offer was made. The state was not in a position to manage their park. Would the City of Lewis do so?

This proposal evoked a general disgust. After years of local effort and fundraising the Conservation Commission accepted Crystal Lake, agreeing to preserve it as a state park. Now they were saying that if the place was to open, the town of Lewis would need to do it.

The council had little choice; for the lake to remain closed, to go to weeds, was unthinkable. The council also suspected if they did not make money, they could at least break even. The *American's* article, written after an interview with council representatives, indicates another incentive was either implied or offered. Hanton concluded his piece with these words: *". . men who are in authority are now arranging for the purchase of additional land for park purposes and it looks very much like the Cold Springs Park will be one that will rank well with any other park of the state in the not very far distant future."*

The city chose Harold Pearce and his wife to manage the park in 1936. Pearce was sworn in as a deputy sheriff, made the promise that rowdiness would not be tolerated at any time of the day or night, and that he'd be in a position to assure this as he'd d live at the lake all summer.

The town's grader was used to put roads in shape. New picnic tables were built. The lake was drained, cleaned, new sand spread. During winter a heavy snow had collapsed the already sagging roof on the pavilion. The structure was partially torn down, rebuilt and repainted. Brush was cleaned, trees trimmed, improvements made to the baseball diamond, to restrooms—all at city expense—all with the assumption that the state was poised to make the promised expansion and renovation of Cold Springs.

The politics of Crystal Lake/Cold Springs was something Betty McGaffin, in the spring of 1936, was unaware of. She was then a senior. Each spring the last day of school was special. That year, for Betty McGaffin and her classmates, it was particularly so as it marked their last day as students of Lewis High School.

Tradition, Betty said, was that the entire school would go to Crystal Lake on that final day. Picnic baskets and sack lunches, brought from home in the morning, were placed in cars of faculty at noon. Teachers drove to the lake. Students walked. The pool was not yet ready, and the late May water was chilly, but there was a playground, a baseball diamond, and the skating rink was open. Betty wore a pair of stylish slacks, brown, and a matching knit top upon which was etched a chevron and anchor. The outfit was a good one for skating. Betty and the class of '36 skated for hours.

The city did what they could that summer for the state's newest park, as did the county. The county road from Lewis south was widened, put to grade, fences moved back, and graveled to the Deep Creek bridge. Park users were asking for more; gravel at least to the south gate, preferably all the way to Highway 48, but doing so was pricey and put on hold for another year.

The state began to move. A surveyor and engineer spent a few days, made drawings and, although they were not specific, let it be known that blueprints were being prepared.

In January of 1937, with lake supporters anxious to learn more about the blueprints, the State Conservation Commission issued a publication listing Cold Springs State Park as a bird and wildlife sanctuary. The message, as reported in the *Griswold American*, included a warning. Timbered areas of Crystal Lake had always offered good hunting, and shooting a few squirrels did not seem to diminish their population. Old habits are hard to break and certain hunters, accustomed to an occasional fried squirrel, did not immediately take notice of legal technicalities. The newspaper let it be known that Warden Mills would be watching.

In their regular meeting of February the Lewis city council read a letter from what the paper called the "Conservation Association." Predictably, the Commission wrote that they were still not in a position to manage Cold Springs and asked that the city once again do so.

Mayor W.W. Trent and council members Porter, Burnside, Sperry and Odem had a year's experience with Cold Springs and debated at length about whether to continue under the same arrangement. Jim Porter, who had pitched shutouts and hit home runs at Crystal Lake, voted yes. Ernest Odem, who had not been much of a ballplayer, voted no. The motion carried, the council agreed to another year.

Burt and Myrtle Upson, along with a tavern owner named Earl Middaugh, would manage the 1937 season. The arrangement had Middaugh getting the pavilion with all profits derived from concessions being his. In exchange he'd serve as caretaker, tending to mowing and ground maintenance. He would also serve as park constable. Upson would have the pool and skating rink, dividing profits equally with the city.

Baseball was not a part of the contract. Games drew people, many of them stayed to skate or swim or dance and that was enough for Upson, Middaugh and the town council. Marker's Merchants had use of the diamond and kept the 25¢ per person admission.

Ledgers show $30 to $50 per month received from Upson, plus two checks in October—one for $948, the other for $626. Although not specified, it appears one represented the season's proceeds from the pool, the other from roller skating. It was not all profit. Upson had to buy skates, maintain the rink, hire some help. The city spent money for picnic tables and road grading and tree trimming. Still, with wages at that time ranging from one to two dollars a day, the gross confirms that the park did a lively business.

Perhaps the most notable event of the season came in September. Under the direction of Mrs. Harry Sherwood, who was identified in newspapers as "the county director of the local leisure time project," a group of volunteers conducted a survey of lake visitors.

The purpose was apparently to demonstrate there was enough traffic at Cold Springs to justify expansion. Some grumbled this shouldn't have been necessary—the State Conservation Commission had promised when the land was turned over to them that they'd expand and improve, yet now they wanted a survey.

The idea, though, was sound. Until then there were few verifiable numbers. Newspapers refer to "large numbers of people." Opening day drew "more people than it had in years." Terms like "one of the biggest crowds ever," and "record-breaking attendance" are not satisfying. The difficulty in getting a count was understandable. No admission was charged at the gate, of which there were two for vehicles. People could walk in from anywhere. They were constantly coming and going. Some were in the pool, at the concession stand; others picnicking on either the lower level or the hilltop. Some were at the ball game, others boating on the river or roller skating or hiking or just hanging around on the beach. They were as impossible to count as the inhabitants of a beehive. Mrs. Harry Sherwood was going to remedy this. She was out to get some hard and verifiable numbers.

Pearl Evans Sherwood was born in Atlantic in 1880. During her 70 years she attended library school at the University of Iowa, organized Atlantic's Carnegie library, became the first librarian, worked as social editor for the *Telegraph*, became a nationally known expert on flowers, particularly the Iris and Hemerocallis (day lily). At the age of 25 she married Harry Sherwood.

Sherwood was a stage actor, an actor good enough to make his living in the profession for sixteen years. He was with a touring cast from the east coast that put on a performance in Atlantic in 1905. There he met Pearl. They were married the following year. She took to the stage and did well. The pair appeared all across the U.S. and Canada. When their acting days were over the Sherwoods returned to Pearl's hometown of Atlantic. Harry was a postal clerk until his retirement, after which he devoted his time to flower gardening.

Pearl Evans Sherwood was, throughout her lifetime, active in community affairs related to culture, health, welfare, education and recreation.

Her survey produced impressive results. A typical weekend in August was chosen—not a holiday weekend or one with a special event. Volunteers were at both gates (at the time many campers and picnickers preferred to use the south gate, which the state later closed for control purposes). These volunteers stopped all who entered, counted adults, children, made a record of where visitors were from.

Between mid-day Friday and Sunday evening 3,706 persons entered Cold Springs park. 2,777 were adults, 929 children. 1,027 automobiles passed through the gates. They came from eleven states and twenty-three Iowa counties.

This, it was felt, would surely prod the Conservation Commission into action.

Chapter Thirteen 1938-39

Upson died, milk bucket by his side, at the age of 62

The town council, Mayor Trent presiding, voted (with Odem again dissenting) to take the park for another year. First, though, they had a problem. Minutes do not tell us who raised corn on a corner of the state park, but whoever it was had secured permission from the state to store 182 bushel in the skating rink. This was not a good idea and resulted in damage to the floor. The council voted to write the state asking that they either get their corn out of the rink or give it to the city to sell, using the revenue to fix the floor.

In April the council took steps to apply for a WPA project of park improvements. This plan was endorsed and pushed by the commission; a commission that already had some engineered plans in place.

Upson and Middaugh entered into a contract identical to the year before, corn was scooped out of the skating rink, repairs made, and Cold Springs was spruced up.

In early May of 1938 F.W. Hanton made a few phone calls. The news, as it always seemed to be in the spring, was positive. The state had WPA approval, was prepared to proceed with major renovations. Hanton wrote that he had not been given "the complete lineup" of improvements, and not everything could be accomplished in one year. What would be done immediately, Hanton was told, included placing a fence around the park, doing flood control, and several other measures that "would be to the advantage of those who visit the park." It was expected that work would commence by late May or early June.

The park opened. May passed into June. Hanton was still not sure just what the work was to consist of, but none of it had taken place. He visited the park on June 19 and found hundreds of people. Many of them were not able to get a picnic table. Hanton noted other frustrations. Restrooms were inadequate. More camping sites were needed. A large shelter house would help.

Hanton was firm in his support of the Lewis town council. He sold a lot of advertising in Lewis and would not have been anxious to criticize even if they deserved it, but in this case Hanton felt the state was at fault. The state was the owner. While the town was making expenditures to maintain the place, it was clearly up to the state to build restrooms, a shelter house, other improvements of that nature—all things the state, in accepting the land, had implied they'd do. Hanton felt that if the Conservation Commission either would not—or could not—fulfill their obligations they shouldn't have taken the gift.

Hanton's article probably had no impact—had the Commission been influenced by small-town southwestern Iowa newspaper editors things would not have reached the state it had—but in early July the Commission released a report saying $11,288 had been released for use at Cold Springs. The WPA had delivered. In addition to flood control (the straightening and re-routing of Deep Creek) a number of picnic tables would be purchased. A wood-frame shelter house on a concrete slab would be built, outdoor fireplaces provided, the vehicle bridge moved, a gate installed, walking bridges, more campsites, a caretaker hired, gravel hauled, additional restrooms.[1] There were more delays. Finally, in September, with the season all but over, a crew of workers and some heavy equipment arrived.

Equipment was in place, but weeks passed without much being done. In January the town council sent a letter to the commission telling them information was needed on the WPA project. When would work resume?

---

[1] Dry privies, of course—no plumbing—but that's all any park was expected to have. Some of the rest rooms, and the shelter house, are still in use. A modern rest room was added a few years ago.

How would park operations that summer be effected? The "we need to know" aspect was emphasized, underscoring another ongoing frustration. The state did not communicate well.

Winter passed. A part of the project was completed, but by late April, 1939, with yet another season approaching, improvements that were to have been finished months before were not. The fence was in and Deep Creek straightened. The new bridge, however, had not even been started, nor had the shelter house. Evelyn Trent expressed her disappointment in a column she wrote for the *Lewis Department* of the *Griswold American* that appeared on April 26th.

No one knows what is holding up this part of the work (the bridge across Deep Creek) and it will take some time to build it and undoubtedly will not be done by the time the park should be opened. This is one that should have been done weeks ago and it will make it very inconvenient to the people who go to the park if they do not have a bridge to get into the picnic grounds. Efforts are being made to get this work done and it may be some real work will be started soon.

This report was followed by another saying completion of the baseball diamond was also behind schedule. Manager Cab Marker had his team assembled, practices were under way, and several games scheduled. But, he said, it appeared likely that some of the early season games would have to be delayed or played elsewhere.

The council had another issue. Bert Upson and Earl Middaugh would not return in 1939. That was one problem. The council entered into a two-year agreement with William (Bill) Jahnke, and that proved to be an even bigger problem.

Bert Upson is on record as having started work at Crystal Lake in 1904. He was then seventeen years old. While he wasn't there every year, he undoubtedly spent over 25 seasons. Why he elected not to return in '39 is unknown. Ten years later, hired to do chores on the A.A. Smith farm near Lewis, he was milking a cow when stricken by an apparent heart attack. Upson died, milk bucket by his side, at the age of 62.

When the park opened on May 28 there was good news and bad. What the paper printed was mostly the former. The skating rink was in excellent condition, the floor sanded and re-varnished, and the latest in roller skates would be available for rent.

Pavilion concessions were handled by Asa Jones, long-time Lewis food merchant and drug store owner. He was, as far as we can determine, no relation to Mont Jones. Jones advertised that his line of lunches, cold drinks, ice cream, candy and other necessities would be such that no one need bring supplies from home.

Surprisingly the baseball diamond, largely due to the work of Marker and his team, was ready. Players found the new field an improvement, particularly due to location. The old diamond, along the road on the east side of the park, had problems with traffic. The new diamond was in the northwest corner, far away from ordinary vehicle travel, and the fence gave it a clearly defined area. Home runs were balls hit over the fence. Ground rules regarding what to do when a batted ball rolled under a parked car were no longer necessary.

The bad news was that the bridge was not yet completed and many attendees had difficulty getting where they wanted to go. Even worse news, although no one knew it at the time, was that flood control—the carefully engineered WPA project of straightening Deep Creek and erecting a levee—would be a costly failure.

The Lyman Hillbillies, always popular at Crystal Lake, put on a show on opening day. They were followed by the Griswold high school marching band.

The band's performance had been planned in detail by the town council under direction of the new mayor, Henry Huffy. Henry Huffy, the man who had been captain of the ill-fated steamboat that sank in Riverside Lake nearly 40 years before, was not exactly a "new" mayor. Terms were for two years. Huffy served several, often with intervals in between. For a time Huffy and Trent seemed to alternate. His term starting in 1939 was far from his first, but it was his first since the town assumed oversight of Cold Springs. Huffy no doubt wanted this opening day to go better than the day he piloted the *Mary Ann*. He suggested payment to the band in the amount of $25, plus "*25c to each member of the band and a free pass to the baseball game and two bottles of pop and either a free swim or admission to the skating rink, provided they bring their own swimming suit or roller skates.*" In return the band was to play a one-hour concert at the pavilion, followed by an orchestrated marching band exhibition.

Band members earned their pay. Following the concert the drum major and majorettes twirled and tossed batons as they led the way to the old baseball diamond, circled the outfield, then marched, played and strutted their way across the park to the new diamond. Through the gates the band marched, across the infield and onto outfield grass where they circled, split and reformed, reed instruments and base drum thumping out march tunes heard all the way to Lewis. The Griswold band uniforms were spotless, the newspaper tells us, brass glistened, maneuvers precise, pennants snapped. Probably not a member of the band knew they were cavorting on land that had once been a lake, marching across the path of the doomed *Mary Ann*. Henry Huffy knew, and must have been pleased.

The ball game pitted the Lewis Merchants against a team from Avoca. The location of the diamond made it possible for a few people in the upper picnic area to save a quarter and watch the game, although not very well because of shrubbery and distance. Those up above had an added attraction. The council had authorized a Mr. Pierce (presumably Wilber Pierce, a Lewis farmer, hardware dealer, tinkerer, and man of many talents), to bring out a pump and length of hose and use his "automatic system" to pump spring water from the spring box below to the picnic area above. For the first time there was running water on the hilltop.

There were a lot of people on hand. We don't know how many. It would have been interesting had Pearl Sherwood and her volunteers been on the case. Both newspapers covering the grand opening of 1939 called it the largest crowd in recent memory. One article compared attendance to that of special events during the early days of Crystal Lake when numbers of eight to ten thousand were reported. The park had drawn over 3,000 on a routine weekend the previous August. If published accounts are to be believed opening day of 1939 drew far more. While editors declined to climb out on a limb and print an estimate, our Lewis reporter felt there was the potential for even larger crowds—that for Cold Springs the best days were yet to come. She also got in the now more or less standard dig about promises not kept.

"Cold Springs Park," Evelyn Trent wrote after observing the 1939 opening, "*is a splendid place for an outing and we dare say the park will be more patronized than in years gone by. We might add that the people of this part of the state are entitled to a place to enjoy outings and we trust the day is not far distant when the conservation commission will carry out the plans to complete the park as promised some time ago.*

Frustrated by the fact that spring turned to summer and no progress at all was made on the Deep Creek bridge a delegation from Lewis and Atlantic loaded several cars and drove to Des Moines. Clyde Herring was then a U.S. Senator. Iowa's governor was George Wilson, a long-faced Republican from Menlo. Wilson, a lawyer and former judge, had been a state senator for ten years prior to becoming governor; he undoubtedly knew something of the ongoing problems regarding Cold Springs.

Like other governors, his private office was in series of interconnected rooms on the lower level of the Capitol. He met the delegation from Cass County in his other office, the spacious ceremonial one on the main level. Governor Wilson was receptive. He should have been. The delegation included Hawley Lynch of the Cass County Board of Supervisors, County Attorney Roscoe Jones, F.D. Simpson representing the Atlantic Chamber of Commerce (and, not insignificantly, editor and publisher of The Atlantic News Telegraph), Albert Christensen of the Atlantic City Council. From Lewis were Mr. and Mrs. Harry Marker, Wilber Pierce and Councilman Ernest Odem.

Governor Wilson heard them out, assured them the matter would be taken care of. Once again lake proponents had felt it necessary to go around and above the Conservation Commission. They had learned that doing so was more likely to produce results.

The Commission could be made to do things they didn't necessarily want to do. They could not, however, be made to like it.

The delegation got back from Des Moines just in time for another major event—the Modern Woodmen of America's log-rolling. The council had been unanimous on this one. The Modern Woodmen of America was, and remains, a fraternal insurance organization. Omaha's Woodmen of the World started with MWA. Iowa, as early as 1890, had over 40,000 members. In addition to the log-rolling demonstration, the Woodmen offered a precision drill team. Their performance in 1927 had been a crowd pleaser, and they were welcome back.

One of the last baseball games of the season was also one of the best. Bridgewater brought a strong team to the Cold Springs diamond and ran home six runs in the first inning. Marker rallied his club, the defense and pitching tightened. In the middle innings Lewis pushed home a run, then another. Fans knew the Merchants had some power hitters, enough clout to come from far behind, and cheered as the home team drew closer. Late in the game Dutch Casady, then the young manager of the Standard Oil station in Lewis, came to the plate with the bases loaded, Lewis down by three.

Casady was running a special on Atlas tires and, to sweeten the deal, he was offering from 15c to 35c for the customer's trade-ins. What he did at the plate was as remarkable as paying cash money for old tires. The ball he hit would be remembered for years—not just for being the game-winner, but also because it was purported to be among the longest ever struck at the Crystal Lake Park. Casady's home run was hit so high, so far, as to make the new fence irrelevant. Lewis score twice more, winning 10-7. His wife, probably remembering how Claud had once missed a game in order to attend their wedding, cheered. And then, a few days later, it rained.

On the afternoon of August 10th the downpour began. Rain came in sheets. Creeks and ditches filled, un-terraced fields lost tons of soil, water spilled over roadways. On his farm between Griswold and Cold Springs, Piercy Forsythe was raising a couple of thousand turkeys for the Thanksgiving market. One fourth of them looked to the sky and drowned.

The state park was devastated. Engineered flood control, which had straightened Deep Creek, brought a wall of muddy water rolling down the new channel with the force of a freight train. The retaining levee was obliterated. Parts of the park were under four feet of water; some of it more. The walking bridge was carried off. Had the road bridge been completed it would have gone as well. Picnic tables were strewn from the park to the Nishnabotna. The baseball diamond, built in a low area where Riverside Lake had once been, would not be seen until the backed-up river drained. When this happened a day or two later the sight was not pleasant. Much of the topsoil from land to the east was deposited on the baseball field. Tons of it settled into Crystal Lake.

The baseball season was over at Cold Springs. Marker's remaining games were either cancelled or played elsewhere. The floor of the roller rink was so badly damaged there was no hope of re-opening anytime soon. Lower levels of the re-built pavilion were under water; silt and debris covered the floors. The lake was not only full of mud that would have to be hauled away, sides were damaged and would require re-building.

All these things could be repaired. The question being asked was what went wrong? A new levee had been built only weeks before to prevent this sort of damage. By this time there were users of the lake who were ready to blame the Conservation Commission for things the Conservation Commission could not control. Phone calls were made asking that someone from the Commission come out and survey the damage; take steps to assure this didn't happen again.

Part of the WPA funded, state planned renovation undertaken in 1939 was the removal of numerous trees, which were piled in the upper picnic/camping area. The young lady on the left is Laverne Hulsebus. Her beau, Otis Marshall, is on the right. Between them are the couple who became my aunt Leone and uncle Walt.

While the rain did damage at places other than Cold Springs, this was not exactly the flood of the century. Back when the place was Crystal Lake, before man-made flood control, downpours like this occurred. They had not been nearly as destructive. Straightening Deep Creek brought too much water too fast for the levee to withstand. Either the plans were drawn by someone who didn't know what he was doing, or the work was not completed as it should have been.

Once again winter approached, and once again those who wanted Cold Springs to continue being what it had been had reason to feel despair. For the Lewis city council there was another sticky matter to deal with. For reasons not disclosed in their minutes, they were not satisfied with the performance of Bill Jahnke. They did not want him to manage the lake another year. The contract, signed by both parties, contained a clause that allowed either to terminate under specified conditions. The council, ready to vote to do so, decided to first ask for legal advice.

Chapter Fourteen 1940-41

King was outraged when he realized the wrong tooth had been extracted

Spring always comes with hope, and with the spring of 1940 there was again heartening news. Governor Wilson's promise to get things moving at the lake seemed to be having an effect. Construction on the much-discussed Deep Creek bridge was underway. The walking bridge was being re-built. Clean-up and repair of the lake, including all new sand for the bottom and beaches, was in progress.

In April the council voted to terminate the contract of Jahnke and Jones. Jahnke had put his own padlock on the skating rink and other buildings he had access to. The city had the locks cut off, put on their own. Jahnke promptly filed a lawsuit.

Mayor Huffy and the council forged on, agreeing to a management method that was less complicated. They advertised that they'd accept bids. Anyone interested in operating the park was to submit an application. The council would review and make a choice based not only on the amount, but also the character and business acumen of the applicants. The only serious candidate was Norman Quinn. He offered $260.

There was some doubt that the park would be ready in time for the announced late May opening. Quinn and a few volunteers made an effort, but there was too much to be done. While students came for their annual last-day-of-school-picnic, the skating rink, pool and other facilities were not available.

Cab marker told the newspaper that the baseball diamond would be ready, and so would his team. Marker went so far as to confirm in the newspaper that he was exploring the potential for a lighted field, and the prospect of night games at Cold Springs was an exciting one indeed.

Marker was quite likely collaborating on the night game idea with an entrepreneur who did things with the park no one ever had.

William Norman Quinn was born the year Chet and Belle Woodward began to build their lake. His parents, William and Elizabeth Quinn, grew up in County Derry, Ireland. William left first, initially going to Canada, then to the United States, where joined other Irishmen who found work with the railroads. In the mid 1880s he sent for Elizabeth. While his work required him to relocate often, the five children were all born in Missouri. In 1903 he was sent to southwest Iowa to do maintenance work on the track between Atlantic and Red Oak. Young William was then seven years old. The family rented a house in Griswold, the end of the line for the Rock Island south from Atlantic and for the CB&Q running north from Red Oak.

A railroader's son, William Norman was a tough kid, an Irish "Mick," and the nickname stuck. He graduated from high school in Griswold in 1918, then studied pharmacy at the University of Iowa. Quinn's college experience was brief. He returned to Griswold, married Ruby Zyke of Lewis and shortly thereafter moved to Villisca. In Villisca he worked and learned a trade in a drugstore managed by Ross Moore.

Ross Moore, six years earlier, had entered the home of his brother, Joe. He stumbled out saying "there was someone murdered in every bed." The ensuing investigation into the slaying of two adults and six children was winding down when Mick and Ruby Quinn moved to Villisca. Moore, by contributing his own money and encouraging others to do likewise, had hired a private detective who kept the case active years longer than it otherwise would have been.

Quinn worked for Ross Moore until 1924. He and Ruby then returned to Lewis and bought a drug store. He later operated a tavern and founded the Central Music Company, a line of juke boxes and pinball machines placed throughout southwest Iowa. He also ran slot machines. Some of them were probably legal. Some of them were probably not.

Opening day of 1940 was delayed until June 9th. Quinn would manage concessions and the roller rink himself, hiring both full-time and part-time help. He'd arranged for another concert by the Griswold marching band. The baseball game would feature Lewis against Oakland. Quinn offered for rent a good supply of stylish new bathing suits. He also set up an archery range and, for a fee, would-be Robin Hoods could loft a few arrows at a distant target.

Conditions were not the best. The day was chilly. Rain the night before left the field too muddy for baseball. Water in Crystal Lake was normally on the cool side—a constant turn-over of spring water kept it that way—but this year was colder than usual. Work on the lake had caused spring water to be diverted for several weeks. Because the lake had only been completed a couple of days before opening there'd been little chance for temperature to modify. Swimmers were entering water only slightly warmer than that which flowed from the sandstone bluff.

In part because it was too cold to swim, too muddy for baseball, the concessions and skating rink did a lively business. The rink was full all afternoon—every pair of skates rented—with people standing in line to wait for a turn.

This made it a busy day for Bill "PeeWee" Ingram. Ingram was one of many characters living in Lewis at the time. He stood scarcely five feet, weighed perhaps 120 pounds, a round-faced man with dark eyes and a habit of shrugging his shoulders, grimacing, and emitting a clicking noise from the side of his mouth. He never married, rarely had a steady job. He worked, when he wanted to, by the day or by the hour. He was gifted with a spade and shovel. Ingram may have hand dug more water and sewer lines in Lewis than anyone else. He also did graves. In the winter, when there were no digging jobs to be had, he ran a trap line. He drank a lot. His beverage of choice was called the "Little Joe." While these bottles of Schlitz held only seven ounces, PeeWee wasn't in the custom of stopping at one.

The story is told of the time he was drinking with a friend named King. Mr. King had been suffering from a toothache for days. He refused to see a dentist. He and Pee Wee reached an advanced state of inebriation and decided the offending tooth had to go. PeeWee got a sturdy pliers, Mr. King opened wide. The operation was not, the story goes, flawless, but eventually an extraction was completed. One version has it that King was outraged when he realized, a day later, that the wrong tooth had been removed.

Ingram was living, in 1940, in a tiny apartment in a main street building owned by the city. We find periodic reference in council meeting minutes with regard to Ingram's annoying habit of not paying his rent. He was not a model citizen, nor the most reliable. He liked his job at the rink in part because he could skate without charge. We talked to person after person who said they had never seen anyone who could skate like him.

"He'd go frontwards, backwards, sideways; fast or slow and sashay around," Betty McGaffin Sanny told us. She skated a lot, wasn't bad herself and watched her share of good ones. No person she ever saw was so transformed by a pair of skates as was Ingram.

He also ran the calliope. The calliope, invented in about 1832, was originally called a "steam trumpet." Steamboats used them as whistles. They also made music. In 1900 "music rolls" similar to those used in player pianos eliminated the need for an actual musician. Some were designed to operate with compressed air rather than steam. The calliope was loud. Even though it was inside a building a mile away, the calliope at the rink was sometimes heard in Lewis.

We do not know if the calliope at Cold Springs was powered by steam or compressed air. If the latter Ingram's job was fairly simple—insert a music roll and open an air valve. In either case the calliope played music people loved skating to. If they went home with their ears ringing, feet tingling, knees rubbery; well, they'd had fun and that was the purpose of going.

The calliope, because we find no mention of it before the Quinn years, probably belonged to him. He proved to be a creative promoter, offering something different each weekend. In July he featured a bathing beauty contest. We truly wish we could tell you the winners, the runners-up, but not a newspaper in the county felt the outcome was worthy of reporting. Even Evelyn Trent's *Lewis News* by-passed the beauty contest.

A cash prize was offered for the roller skater wearing "the most raggedy outfit." Quinn had a potato peeling contest. For the "hubby-calling" competition the wife needed to have enough lung-power to issue commands to her spouse while he was in the back of the upper picnic area, she at the base of the bluff. An event Quinn's liability carrier must have been unaware of was a fat-man's race. No one weighing less than 200 pounds was allowed to enter. There was also a banana eating contest, tug of war, sack races, and more.

News coverage of the first baseball game of the season calls it "the cleanest between Griswold and Lewis that's been played in years." Apparently even under Marker the Lewis-Griswold games were inclined to nastiness. Lewis won on that day, a close, low-scoring game, with Bob Smiley on the mound for the winners. (A person who asked that her name not be used told us Bob Smiley, when angered by an opponent's taunting, or attitude, was known to launch a fast ball at the offending player's ear. Usually the target got out of the way, but not always.)

Quinn kept the entertainment coming. Donkey baseball, music, and in early August he brought on the locally famous "Dancing Spies Sisters." Quinn's advertisements refer to "5 Dancing Girls." This was either a misprint or the girls didn't all perform that day There were actually seven sisters in the act, and they must have put on quite a show.

The seven girls; Ada, Juanita, Georgia, Betty, Mary Jane, Marjorie, and Cleone, were born on their parent's farm east of Massena. All learned to tap dance at an early age, then developed other talents. The children were good enough that their parents decided to promote them as the Dancing Spies Sisters. Georgia also did comedy and sang. Ada did acrobatics. They received professional training. The 1980 Cass County history tells us they were billed as "The World's Largest Girls Dance Troupe." During a ten-year period, 1934 to 1943, the Spies sisters appeared in 13 states, performing at night clubs, state and county fairs, theaters. They averaged just over sixty appearances a year, or about 600 total, and were said to be at their best at Cold Springs in 1940. (The year after their performance at Cold Springs, Ada Spies married "Skeet" Preston, who some will remember as a KJAN radio announcer.)

Newspapers might have been exaggerating when, in late summer, they wrote of "record-breaking crowds" week after week. These words can probably be attributed to Mick Quinn, who understood marketing. Still, he was doing innovative things, bringing in a variety of entertainment, and attendance was good.

Cab Marker did his part. Fans wanted a winning team. He gave it to them.

"Every Sunday," Betty McGaffin Sanny told us, "was baseball. Go to church, hurry home, hurry to fix dinner, hurry to eat." Games started at two. Players needed to be there early.

It was probably in 1940, Quinn's first year as park manager, when Dick Jobe learned to drive a Model T Ford. George Ingram (not to be confused with PeeWee) was the man Quinn chose to supervise most of the day-to-day activities. Jobe, who worked part-time in the bathhouse, also helped elsewhere.

"Monday was clean-up day when we'd go around emptying trash cans and that sort of thing." Ingram drove a Model T and pulled a trailer for this purpose. The car's gas tank was in the trunk, from where fuel flowed to the carburetor. Ingram, trying to drive up the steep hill, had the car die just as it reached the top. He nervously eased the car to the base of the hill, restarted it, and tried again. The results were the same. It was decided the carburetor was either gravity fed or the pump not sufficient to overcome the steep incline. The solution was to back up the hill. A hitch was affixed to the front bumper and trailer attached. Ingram, however, was not comfortable driving forward. He wanted no part of backing up the narrow road. Jobe, then nine or ten years old, volunteered. This was a job he retained until the park closed for the season.

In November Chet Woodward celebrated his 95th birthday. He was in failing health. Living at home with a daughter, Norma, and son, Wooster, he was cared for by Mrs. E.S. DeWitt of Griswold. Chet, who'd been regularly interviewed on his birthday for years, was apparently no longer up to it. While his birthday made the paper, facts regarding his journey to Iowa in the 1850s, his marriage to Belle, the two of them building Crystal Lake, were reprinted from previous articles.

Harry Swan died in an automobile accident in the spring of 1941, killed on the White Pole road.

Those who had worked to achieve a state park, and continued to push to have the Conservation Commission actually make it one, had lost an ally.

Another news story from early that year, this one in May, boded poorly for Cold Springs, although probably no one thought of it that way at the time. The Cocklin Fish Farm south of Griswold was ready to open.

The Lewis City Council wrestled with the potential of dealing with another flood, debated just what their responsibility with regard to the state park should be. What the state had done the year before had done no good—some were certain the straightening of Deep Creek contributed to the rampage—and clearly the dike erected did not perform. The commission, perhaps resentful of allegations that the failure was in their plan, sent an engineer out to have a look. The fault, he said, was in the way the work had been done. Unfortunately, a commission representative said, they had no money to redo it.

The town therefore voted to foot the expenses, make improvements, and rebuild the levee. And once again they voted to approve Mick Quinn's bid. Quinn's offer of $260 was the only one received.

Quinn opened Cold Springs on a Sunday afternoon, billing the park in advertisements as being "Southwest Iowa's Playground." He had animal acts, a baseball game, roller skating, new picnic tables on both the upper and lower areas.

Another attraction Quinn added was a wooden Ferris wheel. His was an old and comparatively small Ferris wheel, but to little Mabel Sanny, who was four or five years old and at the top of the loop when the temperamental old device took a lengthy pause for repairs, it was big enough.

Cocklin's was nice, it was new and well cared for, but could not approach plethora of entertainment choices offered at Cold Springs. Quinn even provided, free of charge and tongue in cheek, a zoo. East of the pavilion was a grove of trees, and in the shade Quinn had an array of caged animals. Attendees, and probably Quinn, called the attraction a "zoo" with a wink. The nearest thing to exotic animals was a pair of monkeys. Children were warned not to put their fingers through the cage.

Quinn, in his second year as manager, was off to a good start. Then, in early June, a heavy downpour sent Deep Creek on another rampage. The dike again failed. Muddy water flooded the baseball field, submerged the park, filled Crystal Lake.

Lila Kunze remembers the zoo and she remembers when the park flooded. Water over the road kept her family from getting to their farm home. They spent the night with a relative in Lewis. She remembers

Irving "Ick" Reynolds, who worked for Quinn servicing coin machines, coming by to shout that Jack (another Quinn employee) was stranded "up a tree with the monkeys."

Water went down, Jack and the monkeys were saved, and Quinn and Marker went to work. A pump was retained, the springs diverted, the lake pumped dry. Stone side walls were repaired, new sand was brought in. Marker scraped mud from the diamond and, in less than three weeks, all activities at the park were resumed.

July 13 was "Cumberland Day." The town went all out. They brought what was billed as "Cumberland's National Champion Marching Band." Their town baseball team did not match up well against Lewis, so they hired a team of all black players from Omaha to represent them in a game against the Merchants. The Merchants won handily.

"Cumberland Day" was followed by "Griswold Day." Griswold returned with their own "National Championship" band, played another one-hour concert. This time they had a vocalist. Miss Lenore Crawford of Griswold was reportedly a talented and popular young singer. For accordion fans, and those who enjoyed a good contortionist, the Wheeler Sisters performed. Young ladies having this combination of talents are not seen every day, and a news account says the accordion/contortionist duet was much appreciated by all who witnessed them. The Lewis Merchants took on the Jackson Colored Giants and, after the game, a free movie was shown in Quinn's open-air theater.

1941 was, according to what Quinn told the newspapers, an overall good year at Cold Springs. The bad news was that for the second straight year floodwaters had caused disruption and unforeseen costs. The state had straightened Deep Creek for watershed control. Both their levee and the one built by the town had failed. More needed to be done—perhaps the plan was faulty—and the state moved slowly, if at all.

The city prevailed in the Jahnke lawsuit—he was awarded a few dollars for equipment purchased and not used—a tiny fraction of the $1500 claimed.

In October the council had a lengthy discussion on the park. The town had taken care of Cold Springs for six seasons. They knew the place, what it was and could continue to be. The park needed to be owned by an entity that was willing to make a commitment. The city was. The council was of the opinion that if the state really wanted Cold

Springs State Park then the commission should act accordingly. If they did not, then they should get out. On October 8, 1941, councilmen Frank Reynolds and H.L Wolverton made a trip to Des Moines.

Wolverton and Reynolds returned, met with Mayor Trent (it was his turn), and a special session was called. Wolverton issued a report that contains the following paragraph:

At the meeting the Commission informed the town's delegates that the park's area and topography were such as to make it an undesirable area for state park purposes, and that they, the commission, would be willing to deed the area over, fee simple, to either the Town of Lewis, Iowa, or to Cass County, or they would reclassify the area, drop it as a state park and lease the area to the town for a five year period, to be operated as an amusement park.

How many times did it need to be said? The original 1919 report of the Board of Conservation, Jacob Crane to Charles Willey in 1931, Crane's official report in 1933, the commission dragging their feet even when the place was a gift. Now, in the clearest language possible, the commission repeated that Cold Springs was not something they wanted. If Lewis did, Lewis could have it.

City Clerk Mollie Marshall promptly prepared a letter. The letter represented the council's acceptance of the offer, included a copy of the motion, and closed by saying representatives of the council were prepared to go to Des Moines at any time convenient to the commission to complete the transaction.

Then came Pearl Harbor. The war, rationing, young men and women leaving to do their duty—none of this was good for Cold Springs.

The toboggan slide and ladder were replaced by a smaller slide shortly after the state took possession.

Pavilion with original bath house attached on the far end.

The new bath house was much appreciated by bathers, as well as Bert and Myrtle Upson.

The walking bridge was washed out by a rampaging Deep Creek shortly after the state completed a flood control project.

Levant Richardson patented his "Ball Bearing Skates" in 1884. They became the rental skate of choice at Crystal Lake's rink. From this building Mick Quinn's calliope could sometimes be heard in Lewis.

A 1920s scene at the pavilion.

An aerial view of Cold Springs State Park taken at about the time of the 1951 dedication.

Savannah Jo Whetstone, a young artist and student in Atlantic High School, captured in oil her vision of Crystal Lake.

Greg Marshall, a senior in Stanton High School, listened to descriptions of what Crystal Lake once was and rendered this sketch.

Chapter Fifteen

The state man left in a huff

The council was distracted by the war, then came a report that the town well was contaminated. A new water system became the priority. Weeks passed without a reply from the commission. Exactly what happened to the offer is unclear. Council minutes following their letter of acceptance, their commitment to do whatever necessary to expedite the transfer of ownership, do not tell us. Minutes reveal that on several occasions "the state park was discussed," so the matter was on their minds. Apparently the commission changed their position with regard to giving the park to Lewis, or at least failed to take the steps necessary to do so.

Chet Woodward died in March of 1942. During his lifetime he'd been an early settler in Cass County, an active member of the Congregational Church, a steady worker and 30-year member of the Lewis Masonic Lodge. What he was best remembered for, of course, was—along with Belle—building and operating Crystal Lake. He had made plans for the preservation of a place so beloved that people throughout the area had joined the cause. Now, with his death, seven years after the land had been given to the state, after an agreement had been reached, with the state having shown little interest, offering to give it back, then not, there were those who wondered if they had done the right thing.

The temporary arrangement between state and city continued. Once again, for $260, Norman Quinn would be the manager.

A curious event took place in June. Some person or persons anonymously reported that the water of Crystal Lake was badly contaminated. The report alleged that flood waters from the previous summer had left the place in a condition ripe for the spread of disease.

While the word "polio" was not mentioned, at least in news articles, the epidemic was real. The nation's president had polio. Jim Painter, who had made his living driving a hack to and from Crystal Lake, had been permanently crippled by polio. In 1942 there was hardly anyone who did not know someone whose life had been devastated by the most dreaded disease of the time.

Word spread that the contaminated lake would not be opened. Quinn reacted, denied there to be any truth to the allegation. An inspection was made by the health department and the lake was ruled safe. There was no basis for the rumor. The lake had been thoroughly drained and cleaned the preceding summer, thousands of gallons of pure spring water flowed into and through the place each day, and newspaper articles were printed to assure there to be no reason for concern.

Regardless, attendance suffered. Who started the rumor? And why? A few years later, when those with a stake in a nearby privately-owned park were reputed to have lobbied against the expenditure of funds at Cold Springs, the anonymous allegations of contaminated water were brought to mind.

Quinn gave it a good try again in '42. He built his own dike. This time, with summer storms not as severe, it held. There was more baseball, although the war was taking young players that were the heart of the team. Probably because of the war, Quinn had less entertainment that year. His advertisements are for fireworks, along with the staples of swimming, roller-skating and the usual drawing card, picnicking, but there were few dancers, singers, and no accordion contortionists.

Quinn re-opened in June of 1943 in what would be his fourth and final year. In July he put his facilities to work as part of the national drive to collect scrap iron for the war effort, which our newspapers—remembering Pearl Harbor—called their "scrap the Japs" program.

The first game of the season was kitten-ball, now called slow-pitch softball, matching "The Omaha Fat Men" against "Krohn's Klowns."

The Klowns were locals rounded up by and named for a Lewis grocer. The second game was Donkey-Ball, with firemen from the Lewis department taking on their counterparts from Griswold.

Later that summer the Merchants, those who were still home, took on a team from Des Moines. A drizzling rain fell through much of the game, which was preceded by a mini-carnival put on by—and for the benefit of—the volunteer fire department. Weather held down the crowd. By the seventh inning, with the game tied 1 to 1, rain came down harder. While Cab Marker conferred with the umpire the meager crowd scattered. The game was called.

That drab and abbreviated contest, after more than forty years of Crystal Lake baseball, was apparently the last. Newspapers do not include reference to any other games that year, and none thereafter.

The following year the state took control. In May of 1944 the Iowa Conservation Commission informed the Lewis council that they'd hired a custodian. They terminated the relationship with the city. Quinn was out. The lake and skating rink would not be open that summer. There'd be no baseball. Art Walter was taking over as temporary custodian. His job, in part, was to begin the work of tearing down some of the buildings. While newspaper accounts try to be upbeat, telling us Cold Springs would continue to be operated as a fine picnic facility, these articles also report the commission's opinion that Crystal Lake, with thousands of gallons of filtered spring water flowing into it each day, could not be kept in a "sanitary condition."

Crystal Lake, 57 years after Chet and Belle Woodward completed it, was closed. If anyone ever again swam there the act was unlawful.

Norman Quinn hauled several pickup loads of his personal equipment from the pavilion and skating rink. In the months to come the rink was torn down, as was the pavilion and the bathhouse and other assorted buildings. Picnic tables remained, but the area was not well maintained.

Crystal Lake was slipping away. The Crescent Club of Lewis took notice. The club, formed in 1909, was made up of a limited number of women having both refinement and social status. They were solid citizens, respectable and religious, meeting for the purpose of discourse on matters worthy of their attention. Membership was limited to thirty. When a member resigned, or was quietly dismissed for failing to fulfill expectations, nominations for a replacement were accepted. If any three members voted "no," that nominee was out and another presented for consideration.

In 1909 and '10 the ladies studied the works of Shakespeare, the nuances of Hamlet and King Lear. They worked for community betterment, raised money for the Red Cross, for the library, conducted drives for war bonds and other worthy causes. Thirty women of social standing in a town the size of Lewis, banded together with common causes, can get things done. Many members during Crescent Club's first fifty years were named Woodward. Even had this not been the case the club would have had an interest in what the state was doing to their park south of town. Ladies of the club didn't like what they were seeing, nor what they were hearing of the state's long-term plans. They made their concerns known in 1944, writing a letter to the State Conservation Commission. Their plea was for the park to be maintained for use as it had in the past.

The letter was a sign of a rift that had been developing for some time. Not everyone had the same idea as to what Cold Springs, the state park, should be. Charley Willey's passion had been to preserve it—not to make radical changes. Nearly all those we spoke with felt the same way. Others, however, including members of the soon-to-be-formed Lewis Commercial Club, had a different vision. They wanted a lake for boating and fishing, a haven for ducks and geese. If this wasn't the original intent of those who bought the land for the state, that didn't matter. Roller skaters could go to Atlantic, which also had a nice swimming pool.

Preservationists believed the commission should have made good on their offer to give the park to the town. Failing to do that, they should at least have allowed the town to continue to operate the place as it had been.

The other side did not favor city ownership, as Lewis could not—and wouldn't if they could—build and maintain a fishing and row-boat lake.

Minutes of the Crescent Club tell us the letter was sent, but make no mention of a reply. The Commission may have placed it in the same file as the 1941 letter from the council—the letter accepting the state's offer to give the place to Lewis.

That summer the amusement park, as the Woodward's had built it, ceased to be. By October Art Walker had completed the work the state had hired him to do. He then took a job with Arliss Trent building a cattle shed on the Frank Retz farm.

In 1945 the park in the news was Cocklin's Fish Farm. L.A. Cocklin, Griswold businessman, had built the place only to die about the time it was completed. New management promoted the park as a commercial venture and, with Cold Springs all but unfit to use, they were doing quite well. Land that would become the Boy Scout's Camp Wakonda had been purchased, but not yet developed. In the interim scouts from 17 counties would converge on "Camp Cocklin," billed as a "Boy Scout Paradise." And rightly so; scouts were allotted their own camping area and swimming beach. Hundreds of scouts, from troops that had once made Crystal Lake their annual summer campground, were now going to Cocklin's. They were only a part of the crowd coming through the gates. Family reunions, church groups, school picnics, class reunions—gatherings of groups that had traditionally used Crystal Lake were now finding Cocklin's. And following a series of articles on the rise in popularity of Cocklin's we find, in the July 25, 1945 edition of the *Griswold American*, this:

MANY INDIGNANT OVER STATE PARK CONDITIONS.
Many people living in all parts of the country are very indignant because of the condition of Cold Springs State Park. No effort was made to secure a caretaker this year and as a result the place has grown up to weeds. In the past hundreds of people gathered at the park to enjoy a day's outing and it was a fine place with ample shade and clean water. Now one cannot travel about the place because of weeds and brush.

The article, no doubt along with a few phone calls to elected officials who were in a position to influence the fortunes of the State Conservation Commission, succeeded in getting a response. It was not a good one.
The "*Lewis Department*" of the *Griswold American* was, as has been noted, written by Mrs. Arliss Trent. Evelyn Upson Trent knew a good deal about Crystal Lake. Bert Upson was her uncle. Evelyn, born in 1913, began dating Arliss Trent when she was seventeen. Nine years later

they were married. The extended courtship allowed (or caused) her to become a working woman, a practice she continued after marriage. In 1931 she became a telephone operator, several years later a clerk in the Lewis post office.

These were positions that put her in contact with dozens of people each day. Evelyn Trent knew what was going on around Lewis. While her duties with the paper primarily had to do with keeping track of who went where, who visited who, the highlights of the school board meeting and Crescent Club and how many raccoons R.E. Anderson trapped during the season, along with births and deaths and marriages and illnesses and high-scorers on the pinochle club, she occasionally had something controversial to report. Sometimes we wish she'd been more diligent in obtaining names and dates, or reporting them, but we are thankful for what she did. The following was written in the edition that appeared August 8, 1945:

One of the men in charge of the State Parks came to Lewis Thursday and made a short inspection of Cold Springs State Park. He also called on a few people in Lewis and from the reception he received one would judge it might be some time before he returns, unless he has something definite to state about the upkeep of the park. It is a shame in the manner the State Conservation Commission has handled Cold Springs. Not one thing has been done and the park is a mass of weeds. Even on the upper level there is no place to hold a picnic of any kind. Around the pavilion are weeds where a Jap army could hide. The people of this part of the state bought and paid for the park and deeded it to the state. Naturally those who bought the park thought that something good would be done to at least keep it in condition for use of the people who reside in this section of the state. One man stated that the man who came to Lewis was quite "Snotty" and said that if they wanted to have a picnic to go some other place. This was resented and the state man left in a huff. We are of the opinion that had the park at least been leased to the town of Lewis it would have remained as a playground for the people of this section of the country.

Mrs. Trent's choice of words when she wrote that "had the park *at least* been leased to the town of Lewis..." indicates she was aware of the offer to give it to them.

That aside, being told by a representative of the Conservation Commission to go somewhere else to picnic at a time when privately-owned Cocklin's was a well-kept place and Cold Springs State Park uninhabitable was hardly a tactful remark. The exchange would, had he been alive, almost certainly have reminded Charles Willey of Jacob Crane.

1946 was more of the same, but Gus Kuester of Griswold was gaining in influence. A Griswold farmer, member of the state house of representatives, he understood how things got done. Kuester was highly thought of—would achieve the position of Speaker of the House—a Republican leader in a house that was more than 70% Republican. He had long stated his support of a state park in Cass County. This was perhaps a conflict for him as he was an avowed penny-pincher—about as fiscally conservative as a fiscal conservative could get. He campaigned as being in favor of many things, yet made it explicitly clear that he believed things should come only when the state was in a position to pay for them. He was a product of the Depression, understood priorities, had his own understanding of economics, and put the overall good of the state ahead of local special interests.

He had also, over the years, seen a good deal of money appropriated to the Conservation Commission spent in northern and eastern Iowa. When citizens of this part of the state complained that it was our turn, Kuester agreed. The war had ended, the Depression was over, people were getting back to a normal life. It was time for Cass County to have a functional state park. Kuester pushed a bill that, during the 1947 session of the General Assembly, appropriated funds for improvements at five state parks, including Cold Springs.

Not everyone in Lewis rejoiced, but at least the weeds would be mowed.

Well, not really. Nearly a year and a half passed. Surveys were done, plans were made, but no work was undertaken. A newspaper article reported that Bruce Stiles, assistant director of the Conservation Commission, said he was waiting for the money to be released, money that, according to the bill, had been released the previous year. Kuester made a phone call. After talking to Stiles he told the newspaper that everything was fine, work would begin shortly.

Everything was not fine. Work did not begin shortly.

Chapter Sixteen

*After two years of Riley P. Clark the state
was moved to action*

The newly formed Lewis Commercial Club had a number of agenda items. Cold Springs was near the top of their list. The Commercial Club favored wholesale changes that included a fishing lake. In this regard they were at odds with the Crescent Club (some of their own wives belonging). The club was part of the faction that wanted Crystal Lake to be preserved as it had been.

The Commercial Club was more aggressive, would have been even without Riley P. Clark. With him there was no doubt—the message would be forcefully delivered.

When Commercial Club president Gale Knoke formed a "lake committee" he chose Clark as chairman. Clark was born in 1917 at a place called Clark's Corner, which is east of Brayton in Audubon County. He graduated from Guthrie Center high school, attended Iowa State University and Tri-State College in Angela, Indiana. In 1938 he married Virginia Berry, daughter of J. Frank and Ethyl Berry. They lived in Indiana from 1940 to 1946, where Clark worked as a tool and die designer.

Not many people are referred to, in everyday conversation, by both their first name and middle initial. Riley P. was. The 'P' did not stand for pugnacious, but it fit. He was combative, irritating, persistent, forceful. His language was often coarse. Clark wouldn't take on a cause unless he believed, and if he believed he wouldn't back down.

Shortly after Knoke gave him the job, Clark and members of his committee made their first of many trips to Des Moines. According to a letter written a few months later, they were told work on the lake had been put on hold because "people in the area don't want it."

Clark came home intending to find out who didn't want the lake, and why.

An example of the way Clark viewed things is related by his son, Marvin. In the 1950s Riley P. Clark served on the school board. He was also a member of a group called "The Small School Association." Clark was among those who firmly believed that small schools were better schools. State authorities were pressuring for re-organization. The word in Cass County was that Lewis would be taken in by either Atlantic or Griswold. Clark, with his faith in small schools, objected. Reorganization would happen only over his cold corpse.

Lila Kunze, whose husband, Rod, was then on the school board, remembers the time as one of the most unpleasant of her life. Re-organization, Rod believed, was not a good thing but an inevitable one. Lewis could and should hold out to the extent reasonable, at the same time recognizing that they could have a voice in making the best of a bad situation, or they could dig in their heels and be told where to go—like it or not.

Bitterness ran deep. Riley P. Clark had a sharp tongue and was not a man to conceal his feelings. It was in this atmosphere that, on Mother's Day in May of 1960, the school burned. The contentious issue of re-organization, which had gone on for years, was settled in one night. While it would be inaccurate to say that Riley P. Clark had lost, the fight was taken away from him.

Clark came to believe the state was responsible for the fire. His claim was that two members of the Iowa Highway Patrol had gone to the school late on the night of the fire and thrown burning flares onto the roof. To support this contention, Marvin told us, Riley P. Clark cited something he said he had been told by members of the Griswold Fire Department. Griswold's volunteer department, along with Atlantic's, was called to help fight the blaze. Upon arrival, according to Riley P. Clark, they found the blaze to be one that could be brought under control and moved to do so. They were stopped by an unnamed person or persons belonging to the Lewis Fire Department.

While the story it hardly credible, and Riley may have been the only person to believe it, the account offers insight into the complex character of Riley P. Clark and helps explain his disdain for state authorities. His animosity over the school incident was rooted in, or at least reinforced by, experiences he had fourteen years earlier when he took on the Iowa Conservation Commission and their promises regarding Cold Springs.

As his father-in-law had been deeply involved in the Crystal Lake park project since the time of Charles Willey, Clark knew much and had a ready source of information. He moved to Lewis to work with Frank Berry in the latter's garage and tow-truck business, and made an immediate impression. He was active—always active—in the church, the lodge, Elks; served on the school board. He had his faults, but he got things done.

In addition to chairing the Commercial Club's lake committee, Clark was the organization's secretary. He, along with Vernon Kuhr, J. Frank Berry and Clarence Hancock were among club members who made repeated phone calls and trips to Des Moines. They wrote letters. How much this pressure helped cannot be known, but after two years of Riley P. Clark the state was moved to action.

Plans had changed. The concept was different than it had been in 1935, was satisfying to sportsmen, if not preservationists. There were blueprints and funding and State Representative Gus Kuester of Griswold so stated both firmly and publicly. Part of the good news, as published in August of 1948, was that construction would include not just one lake, but four. Cold Springs Lake would be, the Commission announced, eleven to fourteen acres fed by springs and windmills. Three other lakes, referred to on the commission's engineered drawings as "major Impoundments," would also be constructed. One, just across the road to the east, would dam Deep Creek creating a lake of about ten acres. Just over half a mile east would be two more; one of twenty acres, the other seven. Plans called for these lakes to be about thirty feet deep and stocked with fish. Plans also provided for dozens of small structures and terraces and grass waterways that would control the watershed, filter any runoff, and assure a lake that would always be "crystal clear." The state acquired an additional 40 acres. This gave them just over 100—a tenth of what was desired for a state park—but a start.

Watershed control was a major issue. About 2,000 acres was drained by Deep Creek. Cooperation of landowners was essential. If the state was to proceed, farmers within the watershed had to agree to, and complete, a conservation plan that included terraces, impoundments, and waterways. While there would be financial assistance, each landowner would pay a share and commit to long-term maintenance and stewardship. The Cass County Conservation Board moved forward with this, eventually compiling plans and commitments agreeable to the state. Farmers who signed on included   J.C. Martin, Russell Whitehead, Lou Kennedy, John Breckerbaumer, Arnold Kunze, Pat Gillemwater, Ernest Osler, Max Saunders, Ben Saunders, Cecil Jahnke, Herman Jahnke, Pete Hulsebus, Fay Hulsebus, Jack Moore, C.W. Hancock, Roscoe Woodward, Wilbur Woodward, Lee Johnson, Leslie Downer, Everett Northrup and Fred Turner.

Why then, late in the summer of 1948, wasn't the project underway? Why weren't funds appropriated in the spring of 1947 being used?

The *Atlantic News Telegraph* carried an editorial saying the lake project was a go—"*perhaps.*" What, readers asked, was meant by "perhaps?" An article in the *American* implies that what Clark and his Commercial Club were told by a representative of the Conservation Commission was true—the local coalition that had held together for so long was unraveling.

This is not surprising. The Viking Lake experience in neighboring Montgomery County is an example.   Virtually everyone favored a lake and state park, but residents of each town had a favorite site. Generally that site was in their back yard. Things reached the point that some were willing to lobby against having a lake at all if it wasn't where they wanted it to be—a fact that probably delayed construction of Viking Lake by several years.

Cass County, on the other hand, had been united. While disagreement came about regarding what Crystal Lake should be, all could agree that there wasn't a better location. It was established, accepted. Advocates were endeared to the place and gave not a thought to starting over or looking elsewhere. Leading citizens of Atlantic, Marne, Griswold, Lyman,

Cumberland, Massena, Wiota and even towns outside Cass County were in it together from the time Charley Willey began his campaign.

But even while the state neglected the gift, as Cold Springs was being surrendered to underbrush, the buildings razed, lake drained, other parks were emerging. Atlantic obtained federal money for a picnic area and swimming pool. Griswold got the Boy Scout camp. Cocklin's Fish Farm was doing nicely. Is it really necessary, some were now asking, to spend money on the weed-patch down by Lewis? Especially if doing so draws people away from what we have? And there was the Crescent Club. Writing to a commission that had repeatedly said the place was unsuitable for a park, telling this commission they wanted Cold Springs to be Crystal Lake, was surely taken as a "no" vote for a lake as advocated by the Commercial Club.

Riley P. Clark cannot have been pleased. In early January of 1949 he penned a letter that would be sent to every senator and representative in Iowa, along with several newspapers. The letter is longer than it should have been. Without doubt his wife, the school teacher, and his historian father-in-law, and probably mother-in-law, had a part in the content and format. It begins with a plea for the General Assembly to look favorably upon the appropriation bill that would fund the Cold Springs project. There follows a lengthy and detailed history of the area, just as J. Frank and Ethyl Berry had written so often. Riley P. Clark may not have been a spelling champion. On an engineered drawing of watershed improvements submitted to the legislature, Clark made this note: "It was decided during the cession.. " The spelling and punctuation in the letter, however, are flawless. While much of the content was not his original work, Riley P. Clark shows up in the eighth paragraph. He writes:

After the park was accepted the state renamed the area Cold Springs State Park, promised improvements, and did nothing–that is nothing other than drain the lake, saw off the pipes that provided clear, cool spring water for drinking, and tear down the bathhouse, skating rink and other buildings.

He then takes a shot at those who had been lobbying on the other side:

In contacting the Iowa Conservation Commission office recently we were told that improvements had been postponed because the people of this territory did not want them. There are a few such people, the owners and operators of small, privately owned recreation spots. It was unfortunate that the thousands of people who did want the park improved failed to voice their side of the story to state officials to offset the private interests who placed personal gain above public good..

Clark, Vernon Kohr, Clarence Hancock, J. Frank and Ethyl Berry, Cab and Harry Marker and other members of the Commercial Club were a presence during the 1949 legislative session. Kuester, as welcoming of support as any legislator, passed the bill through the house. In the senate his ally was Senator Jay C. Colburn of Harlan.

Newspapers hardly noted the passing of the bill, the signing by the governor. The goal had seemed assured fourteen years before, but time after time things hadn't gone as expected. Those who felt it best not to celebrate because something else was likely to go wrong proved to be right.

Work got underway In July of 1949. During the next several weeks bulldozers moved earth, then construction went awry. Apparently there had been misunderstandings between the engineering firm and the contractor regarding just what was to be done. Work came to a halt in the fall of '49 and did not resume for several months. According to a news article published in August of 1950, an official complaint had been filed by the state alleging the contractor had not proceeded according to specifications. There was also a problem with money. Cost was overrunning estimates. The Commission needed an additional $18,000 to resume construction. $18,000 was a significant amount of money, particularly as it came on the heels of an appropriation for $90,000, another for $60,000.

The Commission took the matter to the legislative Interim Committee, a group that had discretionary budgeting authority during the "off year" when there was no legislative session. The Interim Committee was not likely to have been happy with developments, but the project was well under way and they felt it best to vote for approval. Senator Jay C. Colburn of Harlan, who had helped get the original funding approved in the senate, served on that committee. It was he who made the announcement. Work resumed. Cold Springs lake would be completed, although several months behind schedule.

Chapter Seventeen

For all things, Young concluded, there is a season

During construction, particularly on Sunday afternoons, a steady stream of cars drove slowly by. Some parked along the road, or on the bridge, and went for a walk. What they were seeing, for many of them, brought sadness. Sunday afternoons had been the golden times of the golden years. The skating rink and pavilion and spring-water fount and water slide had been previously razed; now the baseball diamond was bulldozed, the grove of hardwood trees that had afforded a shady picnic area, sheltered Quinn's Zoo, was pushed into a pile to be burned. Perhaps most of all they mourned the demolition of their little lake. The one-acre pool; a stone-walled, spring-fed, sparkling edifice that was the heart of the playground of their youth, built with a team of horses, a scraper and boys with shovels, was obliterated by heavy, diesel-powered machinery.

Ladies of the Crescent Club helped raise money to buy the park for the state, doing so under the vague assumption that the park would be cleaned up, renovated, some improvements made. Now, in the summer of 1950, these women were among those who stood in clusters along the road. The reality was for all to see.

For Deb Herbert this reality came unexpectedly. She turned twenty-one in 1940, went to Chicago to begin training as a nurse. From there it was on to California. She did not see Crystal Lake for several years.

In 1952 she returned. "I was in Atlantic and took a ride to Crystal

Lake. I didn't know this had happened. I couldn't believe it. I wanted to cry... maybe did. It was gone . . . that beautiful place was gone."

Cold Springs State Park officially opened on the first Sunday in June, 1951. Organizers hoped to have an event with attendance numbers comparable to special occasions of the past. The day began, as so many at Crystal Lake had, with an open-air, non-denominational church service. The sermon was by the new Congregational minister, the Rev. W. Jay Hazel, who replaced the popular Rev. Arnold Kenyon. Kenyon, although a relatively young man, had a heart ailment and, not long before, had been walking by the Lewis school when he suffered an attack and fell dead.

Ralph Peer of Atlantic was in charge of music. Peer, then 58, was a world class flutist and ocarina player. In his younger days he traveled, playing for years with the Karl King Band. He was often featured as the ocarina soloist. Peer became a regular on WHO's "Barn Dance Frolic," made recordings with the Minneapolis Stereophonic Company, played his ocarina on the "You Asked for it" television program. Peer would eventually make his home in Atlantic, opening a music shop and teaching in both Atlantic and Lewis. Music, that day, was in the capable hands of a fine ocarina player.

Following worship services a few hundred attendees enjoyed a picnic. Afternoon events began with a forty-five minute concert by the Cumberland band, directed by Mrs. Kahla Ford. Master of ceremonies for the dedication was Ed Hamilton of Griswold. He introduced State Representative Gus Kuester, Senator Jay Colburn, and Willard Rush, a member of the Iowa Conservation Commission. These men made a few brief remarks in dedicating the park to the people of Iowa. The keynote address would be delivered by Bruce Stiles, commission director. A few dozen listened to his remarks.

Forty-eight years earlier, from a platform not far away, four speakers waited their turn to address a crowd of thousands.

The year was 1903. The event was the annual reunion of the Cass County Veterans Association, a group made up of aged Civil War combatants and young men not long returned from Cuba and the Philippines.

The few benches provided were filled by early arrivals. Hundreds of men stood in the shade of old trees. National Guard units, brass gleaming, leather polished, were aligned in formation. The older veterans, some of them accompanied by their wives, children, grandchildren, were on blankets they'd spread or chairs brought from home. Many of those not in uniform had medals and ribbons pinned to their civilian shirts and jackets. Regimental flags were fluttering, and one proud old man displayed the Stars and Bars taken by his company in a skirmish near Vicksburg forty years earlier. A few men in the assemblage carried the Confederate flag for another reason—they had served under it. Two bands were on hand. "Dixie," was among the selections and, of course, so was "Yankee Doodle."

Belle Myers Woodward , with her own memories of the Civil War, looked on.

The view from the podium was impressive. Not everyone was there for the oratory. Beyond those gathered close enough to have a chance of hearing the speakers could be seen an acre of water teeming with youngsters. Teen-agers strolled the beach, women in white dresses sat in the shade of the pavilion, concession stands were busy and the stairway to the upper campgrounds packed with those who had the best view of all. Music from a merry-go-round, which had been brought in for the occasion, mingled with the laughter of children.

Lafayette Young, because he was once publisher of the Atlantic Telegraph, had written a history of Cass County, and more recently been a war correspondent, had been asked to speak.

First, though, was Judge Smith McPherson of Red Oak. McPherson, then in his mid-fifties, had been a lawyer, state legislator, and Iowa's attorney general. During college years he'd been a devout student of declamatory. Thirty years of public life, of making speeches as a candidate for elective office, of arguing cases in court, honed his skills. He was a superb public speaker, receiving far more invitations than he could accommodate. The Veteran's reunion at Crystal Lake was a major happening, and McPherson agreed. For about an hour he spoke most eloquently on the condition of government.

He was followed by Frank Shinn of Carson. Shinn, also a lawyer, was witty and amusing—an authentic pioneer—and if he was more entertaining than educational, more about folklore than history, the change of pace was welcome. It was said that an audience could listen to Shinn for two hours and ask for more. When circumstances permitted, he was glad to oblige.

The Commissioner of Railroads, Colonel Palmer, who had seen action in Cuba and had a message to deliver, consumed another forty-five minutes.

When Lafe Young's turn came the audience, which had been sitting, or standing, for a long time, was ready for the grand finale.

Young recalled Teddy Roosevelt, the Rough Riders, then turned to naval engagements he had witnessed. He described the strategy and the battle of Santiago, the rout of the famed Spanish Armada.

At one point during Young's address the National Guard's military drum corps slipped away, attracted by a group of young ladies. According to an account that appeared in the *Standard*, the corps and the girls found each other's company most pleasant. They bantered, flirted and, as Young described how ships in Spain's Santiago squadron were destroyed or ran aground, became increasingly vocal. Feminine voices were heard laughing. Someone did a subdued rat-a-tat-tat on a drum. Young paused. Old veterans frowned. The association's keeper of silence scurried to the offending cluster and dispatched a stern warning.

For all things, Young concluded, there is a season. For Spain the time of being a world power had ended. For the United States of America the season was just beginning.

Applause and cheers followed, those seated stood, the Lewis band struck up "Stars and Stripes Forever" and, although the newspaper does not tell us, we assume the military drum corps and their newfound lady friends strolled off for a bit lemonade and Crystal Lake ice cream.

Forty-eight years later Bruce Stiles spoke for about twenty minutes on the importance of soil conservation. He announced that later in the afternoon Gilbert Wehrman, Cass County soil conservationist, would take those who were interested on a tour of the watershed. Wehrman, Stiles said, would provide an informative explanation of erosion control measures.

Altogether the affair was not particularly exciting. The *Atlantic News Telegraph* did a brief article. The *Griswold American* did not. Mrs. Evelyn Trent was so unimpressed she neglected to mention the grand opening in her events column. Overall attendance was estimated to be less than 3,000, perhaps less than 2,000, and never throughout the day were there that many people at any one time. They came, many of them, to look over an expanse of water that covered what had been dear to them. And then they left.

For all things, Young had said, there is a season. For Crystal Lake the season was truly and officially over.

Chapter Eighteen

...desires to be free from the care and maintenance of certain lands in Cass County.

Many who had known Crystal Lake were sadly disappointed with Cold Springs. Some voiced a concern about safety. Cold Springs was not big as lakes go, but was huge compared to what had been. The "swimming area" was roped off, signs warned swimmers about going beyond. Yet the other side, the west shore a couple of hundred yards away, offered a tempting challenge. The water was deep and it was cold—in places colder than others.

In May of 1952, less than a year after the dedication, the new lake claimed a life. A group of young people from Atlantic went there on a chilly Sunday morning. The water, that early in the season, was particularly cold, but these were young, hearty people and they swam anyway.

At about 11:30 church services in Lewis were interrupted by fire sirens. A few men left their pews.

Witnesses told first responders the victim had swam to deep water, cramped, and went under. Initially there was hope—if the victim could be found quickly and resuscitated. This was not to be. Soon boats, dragging hooks, crossed and re-crossed. An airplane circled, spotters peering into the less-than-crystal-clear water for a glimpse of the body. A crowd gathered. By afternoon onlookers, probably more than had attended the dedication, lined the high banks on the north and west. A rescue crew from Des Moines arrived. Efforts suspended with darkness on Sunday resumed on Monday. A large seine was acquired and boats capable of pulling it toiled from one end of the lake to the other, back and forth for hours. The spillway was opened, water gradually lowered. Finally, late Tuesday afternoon, there was a drag on the seine.

Donald Lee Ordway of Atlantic was born July 2, 1930. At the age of 17 he enlisted, served three years in the navy, then returned to Atlantic. He was listed, on the death certificate, as a construction worker.

I can well remember relatives declaring that no one had ever drowned in Crystal Lake.

Ordway was not only person to die in the new Lake. Michelle Lyne Cahill, 2 ½ years of age, was among a group of nine who picnicked at Cold Springs on June 28, 1975. According to a report filed by Trooper Dick Weideman of the Iowa Highway Patrol, the girl's mother let her go to the beach with a 12-year-old. The older girl went swimming. The mother was resting under a shade tree about 125 yards away. Michelle entered the water unobserved. Her body was found shortly after she drowned.

Swimming continued, as did picnicking, and within a couple of years fishing was good. Mick Quinn bought a rowboat and could be seen evenings and weekends whipping his bamboo fly rod, deftly dropping a dry fly near the swirl of a smallmouth bass. Those who knew Quinn recall that he seemed to always fish along the northeast shore of the lake. There was no shade there, the water shallow. Most found fishing better on the south, near the bluff, an area with colder, deeper water, but Quinn did not go there. For whatever reason he avoided what had been Crystal Lake, the pavilion, Quinn's Zoo.

Ben Pace, who then lived near Griswold, was an all but legendary angler. He was a river fisherman, working the holes of the East Nishnabotna, Turkey Creek, Indian Creek, doing so hour after hour, day after day, from the time ice departed in the spring until cold weather ended the season. Probably no one during his lifetime knew Cass County streams the way Ben Pace did. He did not abandon his first love. He did, however, spend less time with her. The lake was more productive. Pace caught so many fine fish he was tempted to sell them. He succumbed to this temptation and eventually paid a fine—a fine some said was the price of doing business.

At some point during the early 1950s a boardwalk was installed. From the very beginning the Woodwards had devised a system of pipes extending from the bluffs to cisterns arranged so overflow was piped into their lake, then on to the river. This kept the area between the bluffs and the beach dry. When the state tore out pipes this area reverted to mud, which it still is today. The boardwalk was elevated, allowing for a pleasant stroll along the base of the bluffs. A walk around the lake was not nearly as popular, or performed by as many youngsters, as was the ascension of the 102 steps, but the boardwalk was well-traveled. The walk was a good place to fish, and became one of Ben Pace's favorites.

As we have seen, the State Board of Conservation was not interested in Crystal Lake in 1918, publicly rejected the site in 1931, shunned it in Jacob Crane's 25-year report, released in 1933. The state took it as a gift in 1936, doing so with reluctance. They offered to give it to the town of Lewis in 1941. The commission managed the new lake for only a short time before once again seeking a way out.

The agreement signed with the Cass County Board of Supervisors in 1961 contains a sentiment that had been expressed often:

"*The State Conservation Commission has determined that it desires to be relieved from the care and maintenance of certain lands in Cass County, Iowa, known as Cold Springs State Park, containing 104 acres more or less and more particularly described, to wit:*

And there follows a legal description. The agreement, which became effective just ten years after the 1951 dedication, stipulated that the state retained ownership while the county would provide care and maintenance needed to continue operation as a public park. The agreement was for a period of twenty-five years.

The state was not a presence for several years. Then, in 1970, Doyle Adams, an assistant director with the commission, met with county supervisors. The state, he informed them, was interested in locating the Southwest Iowa Fish and Wildlife Management Station at the park. The county's response was negative—there was not enough water to supply this additional function. Adams explored the possibility of a separate well, but found this to be impractical.

That water was an issue, so near to springs that a few years before had flowed an estimated 30,000 gallons per day, is ironic. Water for park usage came from a cistern on the shoreline near the base of the bluff. Dick Mosier, who was park custodian for several years, tells us the cistern was quite old, made of concrete, and measured about six foot by six foot by about seven feet deep. Mosier said he doesn't know if the cistern is the same as Chet Woodward's spring box or was installed later, but it is in the same location. It is worth nothing that the 6x6 dimension is about the size of the platform over the spring box that many, including Betty Sanny, remember.

Mosier says from this cistern water was pumped to numerous hydrants and to the caretaker's house. The water was checked regularly and was consistently pure. During Mosier's tenure people, although in far fewer numbers than a century earlier, took Cold Springs water home with them. (We're told they still do, probably assuming it to be spring water. It is not. A few years ago the park switched to the rural water system.)

The 1970 water issue was resolved, in part, by Glen Durst. Durst, according to his wife, was a chain-smoking Camel man who had permanently injured his hand in a vehicle accident that occurred while he was in training camp during World War ll. Following his discharge he went to work for the Conservation Commission, where he was eventually awarded the title "Construction Technician." Durst had not gone to college, was not an engineer, but those who worked with him remember a self-educated, on-the-job-training sort they trusted more than most who had a degree and carried a loftier title. During his thirty-one years with the commission, Durst supervised construction at Lake Anita, Prairie Rose, Red Haw, Nine Eagles, Green Valley, Rathbun, Viking Lake and others. He knew his business and had a reputation.

Durst did some water-flow tests, after which he told the supervisors they were wrong. There was more than enough water for both uses. The supervisors acquiesced, but only with the written stipulation that the county had first rights. The state was to discontinue pumping should the supply run short. It never did.

A year after the commission's district office was completed Dale Anderson, who had gone to work for the commission the year before, transferred to Lewis. His title was Recreation Safety Officer, an enforcement peace officer position. Anderson would work out of the Cold Springs office until his retirement in 2008.

Anderson remembers the boardwalk, was disappointed to see it torn out. According to Mosier the walkway was popular but maintenance was an issue. He said he extended the elevated walk in the early 1990s, but soon thereafter it was damaged. He was told that, if repaired, the walk had to be wheel chair accessible. It was therefore decided there would be no boardwalk.

Epilogue

Several sources make the claim that Pine Lake near Eldora is Iowa's first man-made lake. The book, *Iowa Trivia*, written by Janice Stock, Allen Beck and Ken Beck and published by Rutledge Hill Press, states without equivocation that Pine was the first non-natural lake in Iowa.

The Woodwards built Crystal Lake nearly thirty years earlier.

Could it be that those who gave the honor to Pine Lake had never heard of Crystal Lake? Or was Crystal Lake not considered because of its size? Terms associated with bodies of water tend to be loosely defined. Where, for example, does a pool end and a pond begin? A lake is bigger than a pond but smaller than a sea, which is not as large as an ocean. One common definition, including that found in my outdated dictionary, has a lake being a body of water consisting of five or more surface acres. If Crystal Lake, consisting of about an acre, was too small to be considered a lake, then what about the basin built next to it? Riverside Lake, also created by the Woodwards, met the five-acre requirement and was completed more than two decades before Pine Lake.

Probably neither Crystal nor Riverside was Iowa's first man-made lake. Certainly Pine Lake was not. Regardless, the Woodwards created a combination of attractions that was, at the time, most unusual.

With Pearl Sherwood's 1937 survey in mind, I packed my lunch on a mid-August Saturday and visited Cold Springs. Her group of volunteers counted, between Friday afternoon and Sunday evening, 1,027 vehicles entering Crystal Lake. 3,706 people had camped, swam, picnicked, watched baseball, roller skated or just sat in the shade to contemplate. Seventy-four years later, on a similar Saturday, I found three people fishing. In the upper campground was one fifth-wheel RV and a tent. I saw two children and three adults. Finding a table was not a problem. I was the only picnicker. I returned on Sunday. The camper remained, the tent was gone. No one was swimming on either day. Even in the heat of an August afternoon the water, a murky green, was not inviting.

   I parked near where the skating rink had been, walked where high school bands once marched and where Charles Willey, unable to see the game but knowing a solid hit when he heard one, smiled at the sounds of the game.

Dedication

Hey, mom—

This book is for you. It's for you for the usual reasons, plus a couple of others. Remember Ruth Slocum? If not, you remember her husband, Darrell, who was school superintendent. He called you and dad to his office about halfway through my senior year and said if I didn't make some immediate changes graduation day would be an ugly embarrassment. We had a lively chat about that, didn't we?

Back to Ruth Slocum: She was a wonderful high school teacher. She told me I could, and should, write. I was impressed and remain grateful. She expressed that sentiment three or four times over the course of a couple of years.

You did so for a lifetime.

How many times have I heard you say: "Roy, you should write about. . . " Sometimes rather than "you should" it was "would you?" I can't make a realistic guess as to how many hundreds of my pages, thousands of words you read and always said it was good, even when it was not.

I started this book with you in mind. Inside is a picture taken of you and the wavy-haired lad you later married. It was taken at Crystal Lake during the summer of 1939. With you are a young man and woman who became my Aunt Leone and Uncle Walt. I've looked at that picture, the depiction of a single instant in an eventful day, and wondered. Who took it? Did you picnic? Swim? Roller-skate? Watch a ball game? Had dad popped the question yet? Might he, like many others, have done so there?

The place you and dad knew was radically changed a few years later. I did not experience Crystal Lake. I knew Cold Springs Park as a good fishing spot and an all-right place to swim, and liked it. The older generation, though, seemed less enthusiastic. Was nostalgia blocking their perception, or had Crystal Lake really been the jewel they remembered?

I wrote this book in an attempt to capture a part of what was, doing so while a few of those who knew were still around to tell.

I very much wish you had lived long enough to read this. You'd have said it was good.

I let you down at times and I'm sorry. Writing these few lines, or the book, doesn't square the account. But at this point I don't know what else there is to be done.

Love ya, mom. Roy

Credits

A good share of the material for this book was drawn from newspaper articles printed in the *Standard, American, Telegraph, Democrat* and other area newspapers. They are credited in the text with references to the specific newspaper and date, or at least approximate date, of publication. Several county histories and personal memoirs were consulted, as well as books on Iowa's early state parks plan. They also are referred to at appropriate places within the book. I chose to do so in this manner as I find extensive footnotes distracting, and lengthy bibliographies tedious. While this may not be the scholarly way, any reader wishing to check a source or follow-up on a reference will find adequate information within the text to do so.

I spent numerous days in libraries at Lewis, Atlantic and Griswold. My sincere thanks goes to those librarians and staffs for their fine cooperation.

Written accounts were supplemented, given depth and color, by people who were there. I may one day go through my notes and make a count of those interviewed. They would number in the dozens, perhaps scores. These who remember Crystal Lake before it became Cold Springs have grown old. Sadly, several who shared their memories passed away before publication.

My wife, Claudia, was raised in Council Bluffs. The amusement park of her memories is Playland on West Broadway. Lake Manawa was where her family went to swim and picnic. Even so, she has tagged along on several of the interview trips, been patient and supportive throughout, and I'm appreciative.

I want to conclude with a brief description of Janielle Joyce Kenworthy's contribution. Her name appears on the cover, and deservedly so. She did not write the book. She did, however, do a large amount of research. When a passage provides a date of birth or death or other genealogical information that material, in most cases, was provided by her. She spent extensive time in the Atlantic library, gathered obituaries, searched the internet. She proofread, offered suggestions, helped with design matters, has been and will continue to help make the book available to readers.

The only problem I've had with Janielle is that now, after well over a year of working on this one, she wants to get started on another.

www.ingramcontent.com/pod-product-compliance
Lightning Source LLC
Chambersburg PA
CBHW061441040426
42450CB00007B/1159